New Design in JEWELRY

New Design in

JEWELRY

Donald J. Willcox

VNR VAN NOSTRAND REINHOLD COMPANY
NEW YORK CINCINNATI TORONTO LONDON MELBOURNE

OTHER BOOKS IN THIS SERIES:

NEW DESIGN IN CERAMICS
NEW DESIGN IN STITCHERY
NEW DESIGN IN WEAVING
NEW DESIGN IN WOOD

Van Nostrand Reinhold Company Regional Offices:
New York Cincinnati Chicago Millbrae Dallas

Van Nostrand Reinhold Company International Offices:
London Toronto Melbourne

Copyright © 1970 by Litton Educational Publishing, Inc.
Library of Congress Catalog Card Number 79-126870
ISBN 0-442-29468-9

Designed by Myron Hall III
Printed by Halliday Lithograph Corporation
Color printed by Toppan Printing Company, Limited, Japan
Bound by Haddon Bindery

Published by Van Nostrand Reinhold Company
450 West 33rd Street, New York, N.Y. 10001

Published simultaneously in Canada by
Van Nostrand Reinhold, Ltd.

16 15 14 13 12 11 10 9 8 7 6 5 4 3

To friend
POUL HAVGAARD
and those who dare new ideas

CONTENTS

FOREWORD

The foreword of this book was written by a young Finnish jewelry designer, Tapio Korpisaari. In response to a personal request, Tapio mailed me a handful of photographs for possible use in this book, and along with them he tucked in this statement as a preface to his work. When he wrote it, Tapio had no idea his words would be published or would reach thousands of jewelry designers and students. Tapio was simply trying hard to get something very personal off his chest about the feelings he had for his profession. He was converting his feelings into words and trying desperately to discover the right words with which to define a philosophy of jewelry design. This is indeed a difficult task for any man, as words are very often a weak substitute for what is in the heart or for the visual forms which the heart and hands produce. Tapio's words are honest, intimate, and spill out poetically—almost as if he unconsciously felt that jewelry design was a vehicle for visual poetry. Tapio is a Finn, a Scandinavian, and a jewelry designer; and since the consuming passion of his life may be in perfect harmony with the reader's, I offer his statement as the heartbeat of jewelry design.

Don Willcox

A unique piece of jewelry is a status symbol only for the person who wants it to be one. To emphasize the quantity of the material and its esteem is to make a piece of jewelry into an investment. But the function of a piece of jewelry is to bring out uniqueness in human character—and this should not be a luxury.

A piece of jewelry confines, seduces, scorns, teases, stimulates. It makes another person jealous, takes sides, is heathen, adored, active—is detestable as well as lovable, frightening, warm, humble, intense, but also calm or playful, or like a wind that goes to rest or the flight of a butterfly. It is as mysterious as the beatific smile of an ancient Buddha, like the sign of dew on a flower, but before all, something of the woman who wears it—her steps on a misty field, the tender quiver of her lips, the look in her eyes. A piece of jewelry complements its bearer. It is something to be used in the same way as an everyday dress, working dress, ski outfit, swimming suit, or evening dress. There is no general piece of jewelry just as there is no general dress; it must not be mixed up with the little status symbols or remembrances that are used everyday. A piece of jewelry is no self-evident thing: it may not be used as a characterless bauble —one that follows its bearer unconsciously.

The beauty that you sense in a piece of jewelry does not have to stem from a routine skill that makes it look unbreakable, strong, irresistible. I think that jewelry is at its best when it evokes feelings of sympathy, gentleness, togetherness. It can be as fragile as ice in spring; as unsmooth as the bark of an old tree; or as wild as the echo of the great forests. Sometimes it may seem timid, and sometimes it is refreshingly bold or satirical. The most important thing is to *feel* that it is your very own—truly and uniquely.

THE NEW TREND IN SCANDINAVIAN DESIGN

Scandinavian artists and craftsmen have long been leaders in the field of modern, functional design. Twenty or even ten years ago one might have spoken of a typical piece of Scandinavian jewelry as confined, cold, perhaps even antiseptic in its insistence upon geometric lines. Today all that has changed. Internationalism has found its way into Scandinavian design, and a new breed of artist has emerged. This modern-day Viking has abandoned the old stereotypes and turned his artistry to the exploration of new forms. His jewelry is bold, imaginative, and unconventional; his use of materials frequently unorthodox; and his concern for form equal to his concern for function. Indeed, about the only aspect of the old style that has endured is meticulous craftsmanship—a golden rule that the Scandinavian artist has never forgotten.

THE DESIGNER'S PLACE IN SOCIETY Behind what looks wild and free in Scandinavian design there is a disciplined craftsman. The average jewelry designer is a highly trained technician. Of course, once the craftsman has mastered technique, he can then turn his imagination loose. His choice of materials is vast, his choice of forms limited only by his own inventiveness. But this emphasis on technical skill makes jewelry design in Scandinavia an intensely competitive handicraft. Before the artist ventures out on his own, he has served a long, difficult apprenticeship or he has graduated from one of the many design schools, and perhaps both. Consider a typical Scandinavian silversmith. In the tiny Lapp village of Kautokieno in Norway, for example, I met no fewer than *ten* design school graduates working as apprentices under one established silversmith! There are, of course, exceptions, but in general the Scandinavian designer, like his fellow artist in America, knows there is no easy road to success.

The Scandinavian market is an ideal one for the independent jewelry designer. It bulges with tourists and export buyers who have a high regard for his craftsmanship. His countrymen, too, love a fine piece of workmanship, and they have learned to value the men and women who provide them with such things. Furthermore, it is possible for a Scandinavian designer to "go commercial"—that is, join a company which will produce his work on a large scale—and still keep his reputation as an independent artist, because many Scandinavian jewelry manufacturers market their products under the names of their individual designers on the theory that the designers' name is more important for public image than the name of the firm itself. Unfortunately, commercial opportunities of this sort are rare in the United States, and it is more difficult here for the independent artist to make money.

NEW MATERIALS AND NEW FRONTIERS Today many young Scandinavian jewelry designers are using synthetics with as much ease and skill as they once used the "safe" materials—gold, silver, semiprecious and precious stones. It is obvious from their work that they're greatly enjoying this new creative freedom: they've lifted the lids off their imaginations and let their ideas spill free; they've come up with designs that are full of laughter, that demand attention, that shout out their individuality. In the pages that follow, many different types of materials are discussed, including synthetics and those traditionally used in peasant jewelry. There is also some discussion of new techniques and handling tools. In general, however, my aim in writing is to stimulate further exploration into new methods and forms and the uses of new materials. Must a ring always look like a ring? Can a designer equal the beauty of gold and silver jewelry using materials like plastic, steel, or tin? I have selected for presentation here what I believe to be the most outstanding examples of rings, pins, earrings, necklaces, and bracelets, as well as pieces that go far beyond the conventional bounds of jewelry design. In Figure 177, for example, is an extraordinary "facelet" by Arje Griegst. Two young Swedes, Bo Klevert and Christian Klingspor, have upset the usual concept of ring with their design in Figure 6, and another Swede, Sonja Hahn-Ekberg, has come up with some highly inventive embroidered jewels in Figures C-24 and C-27. Finally, there are separate sections devoted to men's jewelry and jewelry for the body, with fascinating pictures on pages 110—116.

This book then is a photo gallery—an armchair exhibition of the best in Scandinavian design. It offers the American reader a chance to glimpse at and share new ideas with Scandinavians of similar perspective. Most of all, I hope that it will be a source of inspiration to jewelry designers all over the world.

ELEMENTS OF DESIGN

From what sources does the Scandinavian designer draw inspiration? I've heard dozens upon dozens of theories, some romantic, some logical, and some exotic ones, too. The Finns, for instance, are supposed to be in special communion with nature, receiving their artistic inspiration via waves from birch trees, snow, and the like. The fact is, though, that Finns, and Scandinavians in general, are motivated by the same forces that compel artists in Australia,

America, and Japan—that is, deeply felt emotions and beauty (or ugliness) in their environment. It may be just possible that while one Swedish jewelry designer is being inspired by the vision of a waterfall, another one is succumbing to a creative frenzy caused by a slice of his mother's apple pie!

Inspiration is the result of a conglomeration of circumstances and events, very few of which are unique in national origin and very few of which can be pinpointed. Trees are as familiar a sight to an African as they are to a Norwegian. In other words, any environment is rich in potential source material for the designer who knows how to see with his imagination as well as his eyes.

Nature notwithstanding, the trend is toward abstraction in jewelry design these days. Pieces on political and social themes are not uncommon, especially from the younger designers of Scandinavia. Social injustice is certainly a worthy subject for any artist, but unfortunately much of the protest jewelry I've seen has either been heavy-handed or mere novelty with a label. This is not true, I think, of the pendants entitled "Jesters and Jugglers" in Figure 59. At a glance, these pieces delight the eye. Then one sees beyond their piquant charm the jagged shapes and grotesque forms. The designer has succeeded in portraying with subtle irony the sinister nature of corrupt politics.

There's still plenty of room for realism in modern jewelry design. But the designer who wants to do a pair of cuff links or a pin to look like a bird—say, a pheasant—must realize that he has a very real responsibility to make his pheasant like no other. It should be more than the sum of its parts, it should *personify* pheasant. Look at "Butterfly" in Figure 145, for example, or the unforgettable "Sea Flower" in Figure 143. If he can do what these designers have done, then well and good, if not, then why add more to the thousands of mediocre pieces—pheasants, insects, and otherwise—already flooding the jewelry market?

Whether he chooses to protest against society in his work or capture the beauty of a bird, the designer must keep uppermost in his mind that the ultimate purpose of his jewel is to adorn a living, breathing human being. There are those who get so involved in fashioning masterful works of art that they forget to make their jewelry wearable. I've seen rings that were so oversculptured and cumbersome that they could not be worn with any degree of comfort. I've seen earrings that were too heavy and hung far too low on the earlobe, necklaces that choked, and arm bands that could not be fastened by one person alone.

I remember visiting the design school in Oslo and having the headmaster tell me that each first-year student in woodworking studio was required to design a chair. After completing his chair, the student then had to sit upon that and only that chair during his remaining three years at school. That chair taught its maker a painful but essential lesson in design: imagination is not enough; one must have discipline, knowledge, and skill.

MATERIALS AND THEIR USES

There is a quiet revolution taking place in contemporary jewelry design, not just in Scandinavia, but all over the world. After centuries of tradition, the jewelry designer has finally looked around him and recognized the creative potential in low cost, easily obtained materials—materials like wood, stainless steel, pewter, iron, tin, plastic, leather, and common stone. These materials are not only opening doors to new methods and new types of design, but their low cost has created a whole new market for handcrafted jewelry. People who previously could not afford the luxury of costly metals and gems now have the chance to purchase excellent designs at reasonable prices. And there are an increasing number of designers who are committed to the idea of working with less expensive materials in order to provide the many with items of quality and beauty that were once limited to an elite few. These designers are often criticized by purists for "selling out," but the ones I've interviewed are guided by real social conscience rather than economic reward.

This breakthrough has now gained such momentum that even the usually conservative critics are taking notice. Consider that Finland entered plastic jewelry by two of its leading designers, Olli Tamminen and Maija Lavonen, in the 1963 Milan Triennale—something unheard-of ten years ago (see Figures C-21 through C-23 and 113). And in 1967 the coveted Diamonds International Award went to Matti Hyvarinen of Finland, who captured it with "The Rich and the Poor," a brooch of diamonds set in bands of gold and mounted on an ordinary piece of Finnish granite (see Figure C-17). Again it would have been unthinkable a few years back that a prize that carried with it so much prestige could go to a piece dominated by found granite. I saw this design in Turku, in Matti's workshop, and it is indeed masterful. The designer has succeeded in creating perfect harmony between the natural granite and the meticulously cut diamonds. Incidentally, when Matti and I looked at the piece under a magnifying glass, we found that the granite was playing host to a small, healthy patch of lichen.

Scandinavian designers are busy trying new techniques on all their materials. Precious metals are being tested to their very limits —folded, torn, creased, and textured. Much of the gold and silver jewelry pictured here has a totally different look than the smooth, shiny forms we're accustomed to. The brooch of pearls embedded in molten gold and silver in Figure 142 is a fine example of the success of these experiments.

New methods have enabled the designer to branch out—to get away from rigid, geometric shapes in his work. Contemporary designs are looser, freer, less easy to categorize. The ring is no longer just a decorative addendum to fashion, it is a piece of sculpture in its own right. For some designers, the band is an anchor, and the finger a sort of pedestal for independent form (see Figures 10 through 15). Others strive for a more organic effect: rings that imitate and conform to the lines of the body, like the ones in Figure 8; or free forms that cling to the fingers like living things (see Figures 21 and 24). It is not unusual to see rings of either sort that spread across several fingers or even the whole back of the hand.

Free form is equally common in the design of pendants, bracelets, buckles, and even cuff links. Look at the sculptured arm bands of Bent Pedersen in Figure 122, and Bjorn Weckstrom's cuff links in Figure 200. Weckstrom, a talented Finnish designer who won the Lunning Prize in 1969, is especially interested in the plastic qualities of silver. He has created a series of arm bands and rings called "Space Sculptures," with small figures wedged into seas of molten silver (see Figures 1 and 2 and C-2 and C-3). Weckstrom is, as he puts it, trying to create a milieu in silver—an environmental happening into which the onlooker can be drawn.

Another designer currently exploring the plastic properties of silver is Regine Juhls from Kautokieno, Lapland. Regine's early works were influenced by traditional Lapp motifs (see Figure 154), but recently she has turned to the avant-garde in her designs. Her oddly

shaped pendants are actually many small pieces of silver hammered and then soldered together (see Figures 49 and 51).

JEWELRY—FUNCTION AND FASHION

There are no prescribed rules to be followed in making jewelry. Every craftsman has his own way of doing things, and there are probably as many different approaches as there are individual designers. I offer the following general guidelines not as instructions, but as food for thought.

There is nothing more unattractive than jewelry which looks tacked on like an unnecessary appendage. A piece of jewelry should *fit* a woman. This doesn't mean that jewelry can't be bold or dramatic or even shocking, only that it ought to be built for the part of the body where it will be worn. When a designer does custom-made items, he should design something that is not just flattering, but something individual and personal—*that* is the highest form of flattery. And any woman who buys jewelry must know how to select pieces that suit *her* figure, point up *her* best features, and harmonize with *her* style of dress. A special piece of jewelry may be treasured by a woman like a child his favorite toy. The designer who has created such a piece has every right to be proud of his work.

A designer can work from sketches (see detailed drawings by Matti Hyvarinen of Finland on page 117), he can prepare a preliminary model of his form, or he can work directly on the final piece. Whether he allows for accident in the construction of his forms or prefers to exercise maximum control over his materials, the end result should be a form that *looks* accidental—that is, free. The term

"free" applied to form is difficult to explain. Nikos Kazantzakis has called freedom "a lonely song the wind has taken." More often than not, creative freedom means unleashed imagination. To give the *impression* of freedom is about as much as any designer can hope for: to give his form an air of mystery, leave something to the imagination, something unsaid. Remember the pheasant? Perhaps you gave it one glance and then walked away. That pheasant should have provoked you—made you respond. In other words, a form must *do* something besides just lie there.

Strive for communication. There is more than enough trivia in this world, so why add to the heap? Jewelry should never be impersonal. If it is, then it is bad jewelry. A designer should aim for something beyond mere busy work, something intimate, something that comes from within. Remember: you can be a master of technique and still come up with a creation that is cold and uninviting. But if you are not afraid to invest passion in your work, the end result is bound to be a piece of jewelry that has life.

Be your own critic and learn to be a harsh one. Find out all you can about form, material, and technique before you begin. Then, when you've finished, re-examine your work and ask yourself whether you've really solved the problem. When you have enough perspective to be able to challenge your own work, then you have begun to really grow as an artist.

RINGS What is the shape of the finger? In one of the design schools I visited, I met a student who had been making plaster casts of the fingers of fellow students in an attempt to find just one finger that was round. He had absolutely no luck. Cast after cast produced oval shapes, even square shapes, but no round ones. Yet from the rings

I've seen, it is clear that most designers are aiming to fit round fingers.

After his experiment, that student wrote an article criticizing designers who consider practicalities like the shape of the finger and comfortable, convenient ring bands beneath their notice. Then he set out upon a very lonely path: to take nothing for granted in his work. He and many others like him are now experimenting with band shapes other than the circle, such as the ones in Figures 6 and 27, which will not turn on the finger, but will still slip off and on easily.

A designer who is particularly concerned with perfecting the ring band is silversmith Øivind Modahl, whose work is shown in Figures 32 through 34. Modahl has tried both the super-ellipse (a cross between the square and the circle, first developed by the Danish poet Piet Hein) and the triangle, neither of which turn on the finger. This small functional advantage allows the designer to build very large forms above the band.

Even a magnificent jewel can look ugly when it is poorly mounted —plopped on like an afterthought. A designer using stones or other objects must devise a setting that is first of all secure, and one that suits the stone and harmonizes with the overall shape of the ring. Ingenious settings such as the ones in Figures 28, 29, and 31 enhance small stones and make them look larger; settings like those in Figures 16 and 37 make even ordinary stones look interesting and unusual; and the sculptured settings in Figures 18 and 22 provide a magnificent backdrop for precious gems. Øivind Modahl, once again a master in his field, has achieved complete purity of line with settings that are almost invisible. Modahl's technique is based on tension. Using neither arms nor studs, he wraps his bands up and around the stones, creating a tension in the material that holds the stones fast.

The stone in the ring pictured in Figure 32 appears to be delicately balanced in mid-air. In other rings, such as the ones in Figures 33 and 34, there is hardly a break between band and stone—they flow together into one total form.

Mounting techniques pose special problems to designers working with unusual materials. The experiences of Poul Havgaard of Denmark provide an excellent illustration. Havgaard wanted to produce an inexpensive ring that even young people could afford, so he set to work in iron, even though he knew there would be some raised eyebrows from conservative critics. He also wanted to construct a ring that was adjustable, since he could seldom be on hand to custom fit his rings. Havgaard had decided on new silver for his adjustable band. Now came his problems. He had to figure out how to solder his iron sculptures to the new silver, a metal with a lower melting point than iron. His first solution was to cement the two together, but he was not happy with the results. At the point of setting there was an abrupt break in overall form; moreover, the brightness of the silver band detracted visually from the iron sculpture. Would it be possible, without casting and with only a few basic tools, to construct a ring totally of iron? Poul Havgaard obviously thought so, for he kept banging away until he succeeded. The rings pictured in Figures 38, 39, and 40 were well worth his efforts—they are handsome and monolithic in design. The importance of his work has been recognized by the critics, and his forms are now demanding the attention of Paris fashion designers as well as being on permanent exhibition at Den Permanente, Denmark's well-known gallery of outstanding designs.

Evelyn Noval of Denmark, whose ceramic rings appear in Figures 41 and 43, has encountered similar problems, but she has not yet been able to solve them to her satisfaction. How do you construct a ceramic band to harmonize with the rest of the ring? So far, Evelyn has been definitely limited by her material; her present solution is to cement her ceramic forms in frames of new silver mounted above new-silver bands. One day soon, perhaps, she will come up with a workable method for making an all-ceramic ring.

A few final words about rings and their function. How often will a ring be used? One that is meant to be worn everyday—a wedding ring, for example—should not have sharp edges that snag and scratch, or jutting forms that won't fit into a pair of gloves. Save such features for elaborate, dressy rings meant for formal wear. These may be small points, perhaps, but they are still worthy of consideration. After all, a jewelry designer would be quick to criticize an architect who built a house as a monument to himself rather than for the convenience of those who were to live there. He must likewise apply the same standards to his own designs.

NECKLACES, ARM BANDS, AND BRACELETS Jewelry worn around the neck or on the arm should be light and comfortable. When such jewelry is too heavy or bulky, a woman may be made to feel like a slave weighted down with chains. A well-designed necklace or bracelet should also be manageable—easy to open and close *without* assistance. Designers who aim for a totally sculptured look often conceal their fasteners (as in Figures 67 and 125) or incorporate them into the overall design (see Figures 79 and 84). An alternate solution is to dispense with them entirely, the way the designer of the necklace in Figure 70 has done.

Loose-fitting bracelets like the one in Figure 126 are usually worn at the wrist; while adjustable pieces (such as Figure 127) and open arm bands (Figures 129 and 130) fit neatly anywhere on the arm. Pendants are generally hung from the neck by a chain or formed wire. Classic examples are the ones in Figures 72 and 76, where the chains are little more than devices to hold the ornaments to the body. Necklaces of the type featured in Figures 55 and 62 are of a more continuous design. Other variations include the sculptured necklace pictured in Figure 57 and the streamlined "choker" in Figure 68, with links at the back to permit opening and closing without bending. A striking version of the close-fitting neck band is the gold collar in Figure 88, which resembles a man's bow tie. Also worthy of special note are the pieces done in nontraditional materials, for example, the leather pendants in Figure 109 and the pewter designs featured in Figures 93 and 95 through 104.

EARRINGS AND HEAD ORNAMENTS As with other kinds of jewelry, weight is an essential consideration in earring design. A too-heavy earring is painful to wear, and if the ear is not pierced, it is likely to wind up on the floor. Designers should also avoid sharp, jagged edges and remember that objects dangling from the ear should be properly balanced to limit their motion.

Examples of hanging earrings in intriguing shapes are the free forms in Figures 158 and 160. Birgitta Haeggbom of Sweden and Tone Vigeland of Norway are two designers who have enlarged on this popular motif. Their captivating ear jewels are seen in Figures 155 and 157.

Interesting items to ornament the hair and ears are the pieces designed by Paula Haivaoja and Cecilia Johansson, both of Sweden (see Figures 169 and 171). Another striking new design is the silver headpiece seen in Figure 170, which is worn like a hat over the top of the head.

BUCKLES AND JEWELRY FOR THE BODY The waist is curved, and any large piece designed to be worn at the waist must curve with it. It is complete nonsense to design long, flat buckles that project out from the body and catch on everything nearby. For the same practical reason, the surface of buckles should be fairly smooth. Outstanding examples of attractive and functional designs are Poul Havgaard's buckles in Figures 181 through 184 and 186 and 187, which curve slightly to the waist and are hollowed out at the back to reduce their weight. Belt loops and studs fit neatly together on the reverse side to give the buckles a totally sculptured look.

Body jewels, especially chain belts and other elaborate waist ornaments, have become enormously popular during the past few years. A bit more avant-garde, perhaps, are the breast pieces designed by Poul Havgaard in Figures 190, 192, and 193 and his navel ornaments in Figures 191 and C-18.

MEN'S JEWELRY During the past decade, men's fashions have changed at least as radically as women's, and with this result: decorative jewelry is no longer exclusively a feminine domain. Today a man can choose from a wide range of styles in cuff links and tie clips, as well as fancy rings and watch bands and neck jewelry designed especially for him. Many of the rings and pendants featured in this book can be worn equally well by men and women. In addition, some forward-looking Scandinavian designers have come up with the "antie" (see Figures 194 through 196), which may one day replace the traditional necktie in man's wardrobe.

SUMMARY: A WORD TO THE CONSERVATIVE

Oh my! I wonder, is the skeptical reader sitting back right now and asking himself bemusedly what jewelry design is coming to? Is he muttering to himself, "Since when are buckles classified as jewelry?" Or, "Who would really take a plastic ring seriously?" Or is he opening his eyes, taking an honest look at these new designs, and suddenly realizing that it all works! That plastic, glass, steel, are materials that typify this age of technology we live in. That free form may be the symbolic language of this generation of artists. That in this day of relaxed styles there can be few limits on personal adornment. Anything, even mundane things like snaps, hooks, and zippers, is fair game for the jewelry designer.

The death of tradition—the notion that only certain materials and certain styles are acceptable in jewelry design— has gone unmourned among contemporary designers. If there are still those who refuse to take the new forms seriously, their voices are growing dimmer, and the young designers with new ideas have learned to ignore their criticism. As for the public, especially the young, they are anything but conservative in their tastes. Walk down the streets of any large city and look in the shops and you will realize that people are willing and eager to buy unusual and avant-garde designs.

The jewelry designer with original ideas today never need fear public scorn. He can respond to the demands of the consumer and still follow the dictates of his own artistic conscience. He knows, like Tapio Korpisaari, that "a piece of jewelry is no self-evident thing: it may not be used as a characterless bauble—one that follows its bearer unconsciously." Thus he has cast busy work aside and faced the real challenge—to create a piece of jewelry that will mean something to the individual who owns it, that will be unique, that will have *soul.*

C-1. Arm band in silver with stones against a background of contrasting surfaces. By Olle Ohlsson of Sweden. (Courtesy of Kollegiet for Sverige—Information.)

C-2. "Near Eruption," silver ring from "Space Sculpture" series by Bjorn Weckstrom of Finland. (Courtesy of Lapponia Jewelry Ltd.)

C-3. "Ikaros," silver ring symbolizing flight. From series entitled "Space Sculpture" by Biorn Weckstrom of Finland. (Courtesy of Lapponia Jewelry Ltd.)

C-4. Two necklaces from dyed birch beads by Kaija Aarikka of Finland. The beads are given a satin finish by buffing them on a wheel coated with paraffin.

C-1 C-2

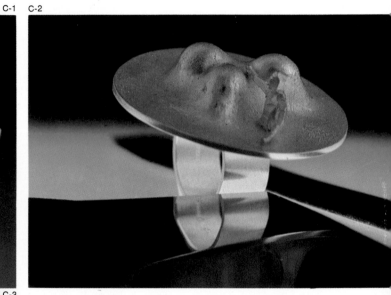

C-3

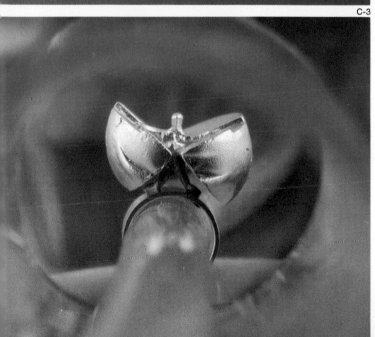

C-4

C-5. "Ode to Henry Moore," arm band in gold by Bjorn Weckstrom of Finland. (Courtesy of Lapponia Jewelry Ltd.)

C-6. "Bird God," gold pendant with tourmaline grains by Bjorn Weckstrom of Finland. The inspiration for this piece was the white skeleton of a bird, which Weckstrom found in the sea. (Courtesy of Lapponia Jewelry Ltd.)

C-7. Hammer-shaped amulet (Tor's hammer) made of powdered silver and dating from the tenth century. Tor was the god of weather and one of the three main gods of Norse myth, along with Oden (the god of war) and Freyja (the god of fertility). (Courtesy of Historiska Museet, Stockholm.)

C-5

C-6

C-7

C-8

C-9

C-10

C-11

C-12

C-13

C-14. Arm band of crocheted silver thread by Rolf Grude of Norway. This design was an experiment by Grude to create what he calls a "living surface." (Courtesy of *Bonytt* magazine.)

C-15. Silver pendant by Per Bjurtoft of Sweden. The form was cast in wax and then set within a polished shell. (Courtesy of Kollegiet for Sverige—Information.)

C-16. Brass necklaces cut from sheet brass. By Seppo Tamminen of Finland. (Courtesy of Merkki Sorsa Oy.)

C-17. "The Rich and the Poor," brooch in diamonds, gold, and Finnish red granite. By Matti Hyvarinen of Finland.

C-18. "Belly Brooch" in silver with smoke quartz. By Rolf Grude of Norway.

C-19. Pendant of molten gold, pearls, and red granite. By Matti Hyvarinen of Finland.

C-20. Brooch by Matti Hyvarinen of Finland. This design was inspired by the wild flowers seen grouped around it.

C-15   C-16

C-21

C-22

C-23

C-24

C-25

C-21. Acrylic arm band by Olli Tamminen of Finland.

C-22. Laminated acrylic ring by Olli Tamminen of Finland.

C-23. Laminated acrylic arm band by Olli Tamminen of Finland.

C-24. Embroidered brooch of yarn, gold thread, and pearls. By Sonja Hahn-Ekberg of Sweden. (Courtesy of Svenska Slojdforeningen.)

C-25. Silver arm band with two silver rings. By Sigrid and Inge Hoyvik of Norway.

C-26. Silver rings by Kaija Aarikka of Finland.

C-27. Embroidered necklace by Sonja Hahn-Ekberg of Sweden. The designer begins with a cardboard form, over which she embroiders with linen yarn, silver and gold thread, and glass beads.

C-28. "An Item From Vorga," silver ring by Bjorn Weckstrom of Finland. (Courtesy of Lapponia Jewelry Ltd.)

C-29. Necklace combining gold and silver by Olle Ohlsson of Sweden. (Courtesy of Kollegiet for Sverige—Information.)

C-28

C-29

RINGS

1. Silver ring from series entitled "Space Sculpture" by Bjorn Weckstrom of Finland. (Courtesy of Kruunu Koru Oy.)

2. Another silver ring from "Space Sculpture" series. Weckstrom defines this form as an environment in silver where, through the technique of folding, he explores the plasticity of silver. (Courtesy of Kruunu Koru Oy.)

1

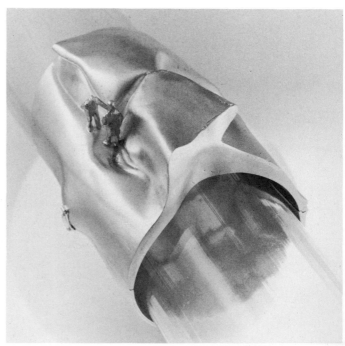

2

3. Hammered silver ring by Olle Ohlsson of Sweden. (Courtesy of Kollegiet for Sverige—Information.)

4. Silver ring made from silver wire by Pirkko Lahteenmaki of Finland. (Courtesy of the Finnish Society of Crafts and Design.)

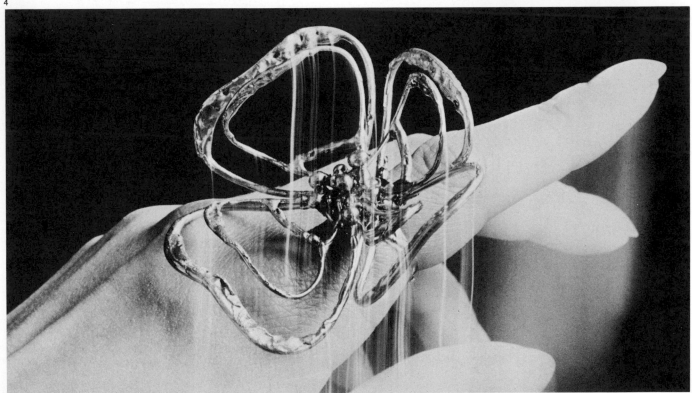

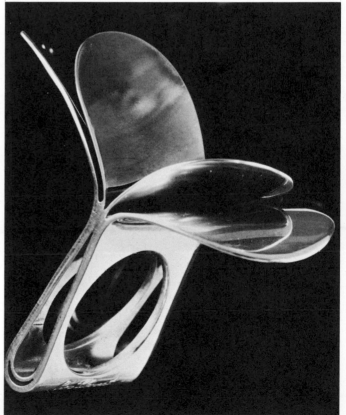

5. This silver ring by Thor Selzer of Denmark has a "constructed" look. It is set with two opal matrixes and one tourmaline. (Courtesy of the Danish Society of Arts and Crafts.)

6. Silver ring by Bo Klevert and Christian Klingspor of Sweden. An attempt by two young designers to redefine the band shape of a ring. (Courtesy of *Sweden Now* magazine.)

7. Silver ring with gold balls by Ole Kjaer Jensen of Denmark. Although it looks like it might be unsteady, the balls are positioned to prevent the ring from turning.

8. Three silver rings by Paula Haivaoja of Finland. Note the open band form on all of these rings. (Courtesy of Kalevala Koru Oy.)

9. A selection of silver rings in bold forms by Kaija Aarikka of Finland.

7
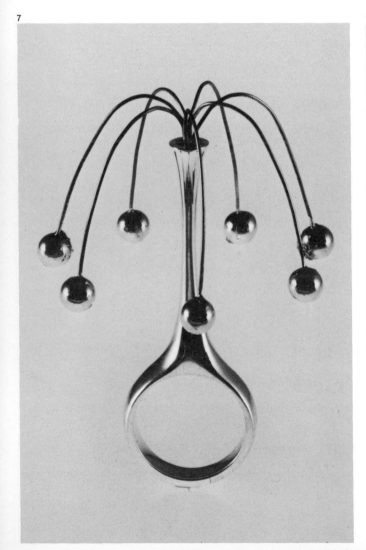

8

10. Therapy ring in silver for "ex-users of LSD" by Tapio Korpisaari of Finland.

11–12. Silver rings with beach stones by Tapio Korpisaari of Finland.

13. Therapy rings in silver for "ex-users of LSD" by Tapio Korpisaari of Finland. Each of these rings has a hinged cover —a "pill box."

14. Silver ring by Tapio Korpisaari of Finland. Note the split band form.

11

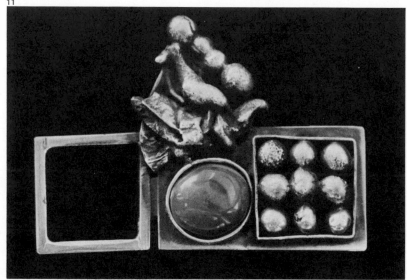

10

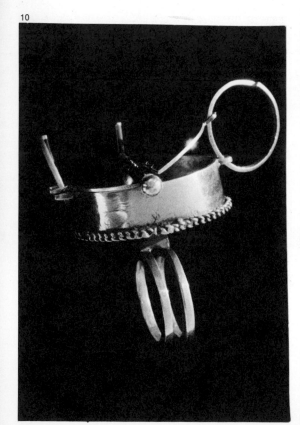

12

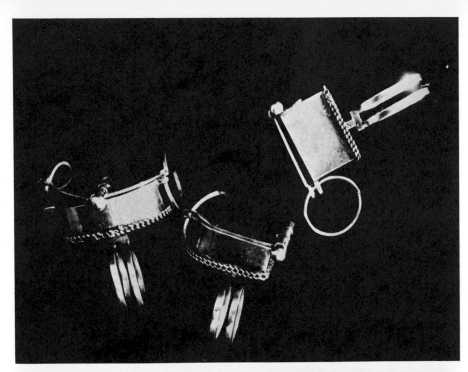

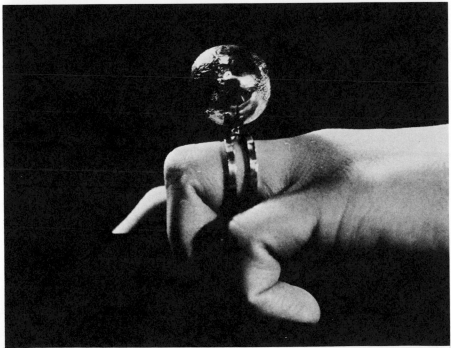

15. Ring combining silver and gold by Mirjam Salminen of Finland. (Courtesy of Kaunis Koru Oy.)

16. Silver ring with suspended turquoise ball by Helga and Bent Exner of Denmark. (Courtesy of the Danish Society of Arts and Crafts.)

17. Silver ring with pendants by Helga and Bent Exner of Denmark. (Courtesy of the Danish Society of Arts and Crafts.)

15

16

17

18

19

20

18. Sculptured gold ring set with pearls, diamonds, and amethysts. By Arje Griegst of Denmark. (Courtesy of the Danish Society of Arts and Crafts.)

19. Silver ring with mushroom forms by Saara Hopea of Finland (Courtesy of the Finnish Society of Crafts and Design.)

20. Traditional Lapp silver rings. (Courtesy of the National Museum of Finland.)

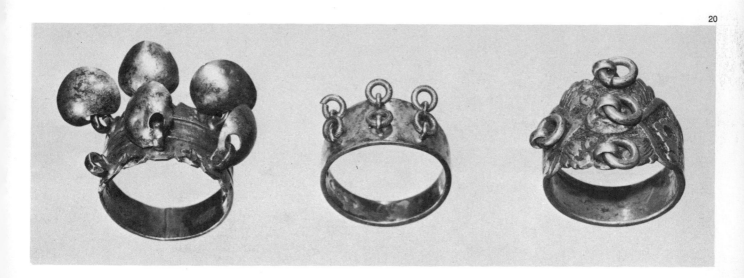

21. Free-form gold ring set with diamonds and pearls by Arje Griegst of Denmark. The band is a sculptured part of the ring form and prevents it from turning. (Courtesy of the Danish Society of Arts and Crafts.)

22. Two rings by Marianne Aulin and Willy Paldan of Denmark: (a) "A Leaf of Kale," 18-karat gold ring with three white pearls; (b) "The Hobbit," 18-karat gold ring with two white pearls and one black pearl.

21

22

a   b

23. "The Ray," 18-karat gold ring by Marianne Aulin and Willy Paldan of Denmark. The surface here is textured.

24. Two more rings by Marianne Aulin and Willy Paldan of Denmark: (a) "The Ring of Eyes," 18-karat gold. In "The Ring of Eyes," the theme has been carried down into the band to create the effect of total form. (b) "The Mistletoe," 18-karat gold ring with five opals.

23

24

a

b

25. "Ladybird," gold and silver ring by Liisa Vitali of Finland. (Courtesy of the Finnish Society of Crafts and Design.)

26. Gold ring has a pattern of repeated half circles and small rings. By Bjorn Ostern of Norway. (Courtesy of *Bonytt* magazine.)

27. Hammered red-gold ring with three diamonds by Elon Arenhill of Sweden. The shape of the band prevents the ring from turning.

26

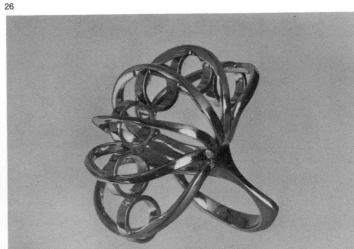

25

27

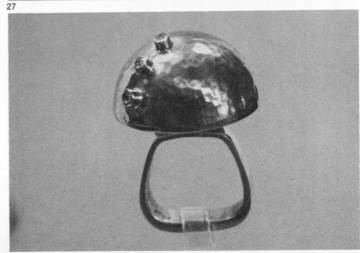

28. Fourteen-karat gold ring with brilliant-cut diamonds set in palladium. By Elis Kauppi of Finland. (Courtesy of Kupittaan Kulta Oy.)

29. Fourteen-karat gold ring with brilliant-cut diamonds in palladium setting. By Elis Kauppi of Finland. (Courtesy of Kupittaan Kulta Oy.)

28

29

30. Gold ring made from wire by Anders Hogberg of Sweden. (Courtesy of Kollegiet for Sverige—Information.)

31. Eighteen-karat gold ring with brilliants by Kerstin Ohlin Lejonklou of Sweden. (Courtesy of Kollegiet for Sverige—Information.)

32

33

32. Gold ring with large turquoise by Øivind Modahl of Norway. This stone is held in place entirely by the tension created in the band.

33. Silver ring with crystals of amethyst by Øivind Modahl of Norway.

34. Three silver rings by Øivind Modahl of Norway. The stones are all held by tension. Left: red quartz; center: amethyst; right: amazonite.

34

35. Fourteen-karat gold band with rock crystals by Bent Knudsen of Denmark. (Courtesy of the Royal Danish Ministry for Foreign Affairs.)

36. Engraved tiger shell ring by Matti Hyvarinen of Finland. The subject of the engraved portrait—the designer's sister—can be seen in the background. (Courtesy of Sirokoru.)

37. Unusual side mounting on silver band by Ole W. Jacobsen of Denmark. (Courtesy of the Danish Society of Arts and Crafts.)

38. Iron ring by Poul Havgaard of Denmark. This finger sculpture was built with an acetylene torch, burned with cutting oil to induce black areas, and then the contrasting silver-like surfaces were smoothed with emery paper and steel wool. The large form is prevented from turning by the lips that extend out above the adjacent fingers.

35

36

37

38

39

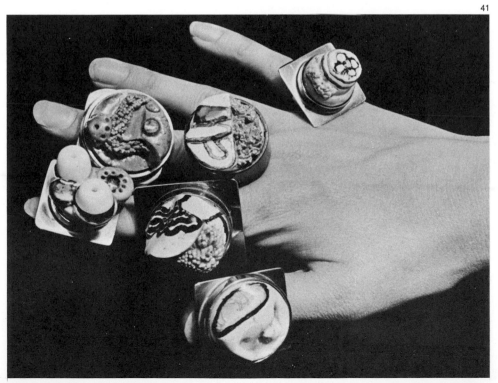

40

41

39. Sculptured iron ring by Poul Havgaard of Denmark. The iron does eventually rust, especially if subjected to salt water, but it requires no more care than ordinary silver to maintain the smooth surfaces. An extra-fine piece of steel wool keeps it rust free.

40. Iron ring by Poul Havgaard of Denmark. The designer is now working with several chemical firms to find epoxy resins which can be coated on the iron surface to permanently prevent rust.

41. Ceramic sculptures cemented in new-silver band frames by Evelyn Noval of Denmark. Miss Noval has also tried using band frames of copper, brass, and iron.

42. Free-form iron ring by Poul Havgaard of Denmark. The open band is adjustable.

43. Ceramic rings (detail) by Evelyn Noval of Denmark.

42

43

44. "Sieve Ring" of stainless steel by Rita Salo of Finland. (Courtesy of Marimekko Oy.)

45. "Mirror Ring" of stainless steel by Rita Salo of Finland. The open band is adjustable. (Courtesy of Marimekko Oy.)

44

46. Plastic rings by Siv Lagerstrom of Sweden. The cubes of transparent plastic create liquid-like frames for the colored center pins.

47. Laminated acrylic ring by Olli Tamminen of Finland.

48. Organic free-form reindeer-horn ring by Olli Tamminen of Finland. In the summer of 1968, together with several other Finnish designers, Tamminen devoted time to teaching Lapps what they could do with the material on hand. This carved ring was one result.

46

47

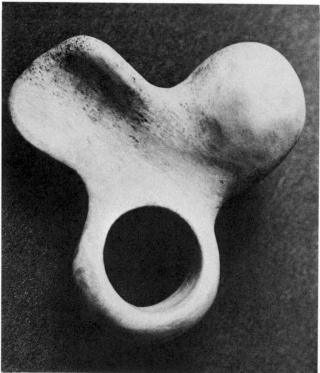

48

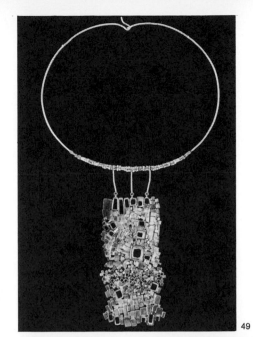

49

PENDANTS AND NECKLACES

49. Silver pendant by Regine Juhls of Norway. Uneven surface texture was obtained by soldering together several dozen individual pieces of silver.

50. Silver pendant made from silver wire by Pirkko Lahteenmaki of Finland. (Courtesy of the Finnish Society of Crafts and Design.)

50

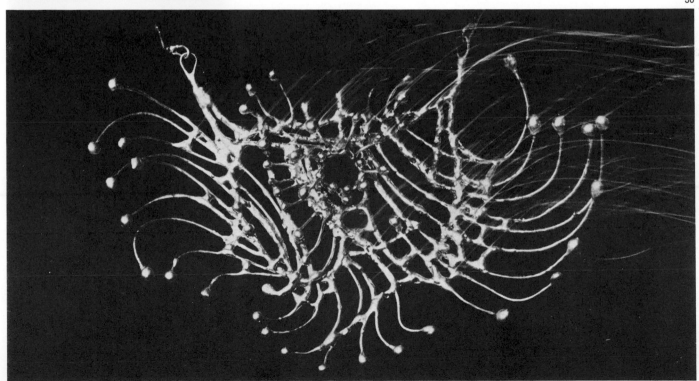

51. Soldered silver pendant by Regine Juhls of Norway.

52. "A Cherry From Under The Snow," silver pendant by Tapio Korpisaari of Finland.

53. "The Water Awakens," silver necklace with beach stones (matching ring shown in center). By Tapio Korpisaari of Finland.

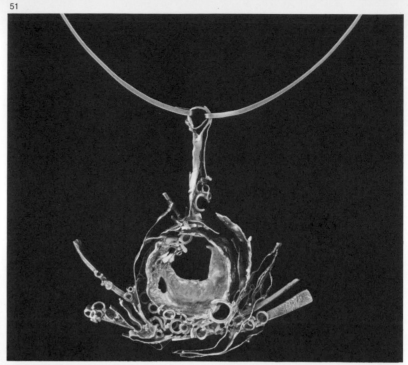

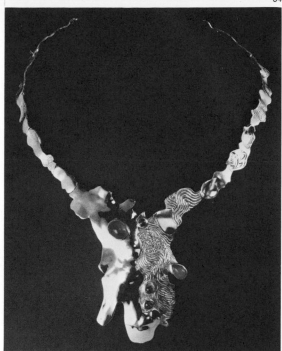

54. Necklace of gold and silver by Olle Ohlsson of Sweden. Rough and smooth surfaces are combined for textured effect. Stones are blue topaz and pink tourmaline. (Courtesy of Kollegiet for Sverige—Information.)

55. Sculptured necklace of gold and silver with six emeralds by Olle Ohlsson of Sweden. (Courtesy of Kollegiet for Sverige—Information.)

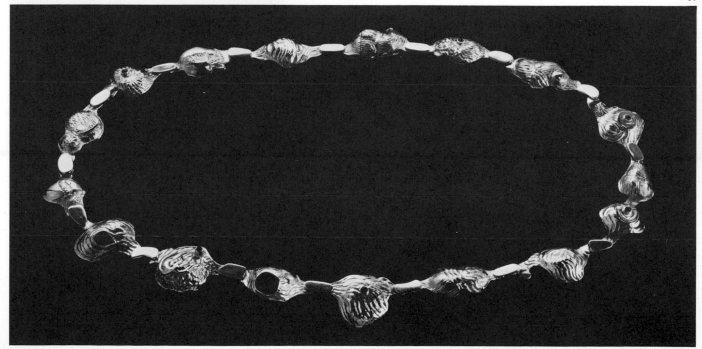

56. Silver necklace made from flat silver strips. By Per Arne Terrs Lundahl of Sweden. (Courtesy of Svenska Slojdforeningen.)

57. Gold and silver necklace with textured surface by Olle Ohlsson of Sweden. (Courtesy of Kollegiet for Sverige—Information.)

58. Silver necklace with aquamarines, citrines, and tourmalines by Olle Ohlsson of Sweden. Surface texturing is repeated throughout. Continuous form gives necklace a totally sculptured look. (Courtesy of Kollegiet for Sverige—Information.)

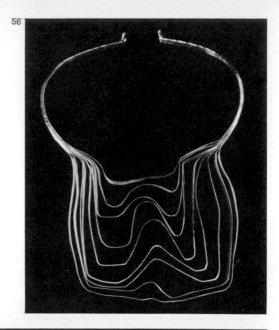

56

58

57

59. Silver pendants from a series entitled "Jesters And Jugglers" by Owe Johansson of Sweden. (Courtesy of Kollegiet for Sverige—Information.)

59

60. Silver pendant with mixed stones by
Sigrid and Inge Høivik of Norway. (Courtesy
of *Bonytt* magazine.)

61. Silver necklace of turquoise against a
textured and beaded surface. By Bent
Gabrielsen Pedersen of Denmark. (Courtesy
of Hans Hansen and the Danish Society of
Arts and Crafts.)

62. Necklace of enameled silver by Arje
Griegst of Denmark. (Courtesy of the Danish
Society of Arts and Crafts.)

60

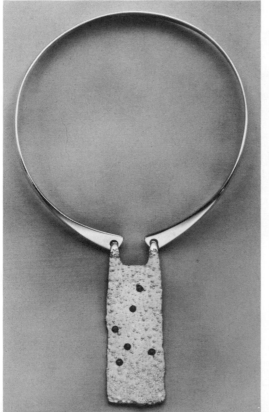

61

62

63. Silver pendant with hammered necklace by Erling Christophersen of Norway. (Courtesy of Norway Designs.)

64. Silver pendant by Mirjam Salminen of Finland. (Courtesy of Kaunis Koru Oy.)

65. Silver necklace of wheels by Paula Haivaoja of Finland. (Courtesy of Kalevala Koru.)

66. Silver pendant with rotating ball by Helga and Bent Exner of Denmark. (Courtesy of Den Permanente.)

67. Silver necklace designed by Nanna and Jørgen Ditzel of Denmark for Georg Jensen Silversmiths Ltd. (Courtesy of the Danish Society of Arts and Crafts.)

68. Firegilt necklace in silver by Bent Gabrielsen Pedersen of Denmark. (Courtesy of Hans Hansen and the Danish Society of Arts and Crafts.)

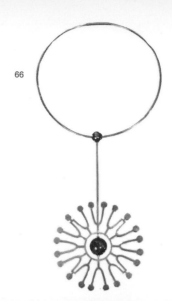

66

67

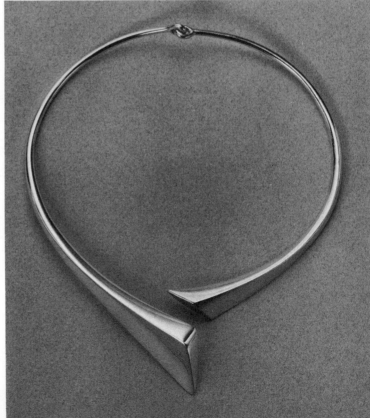

68

69. Silver necklace with mobile by Anni and Bent Knudsen of Denmark. (Courtesy of the Royal Danish Ministry for Foreign Affairs.)

70. Necklace with amber by Arje Griegst of Denmark. (Courtesy of the Danish Society of Arts and Crafts.)

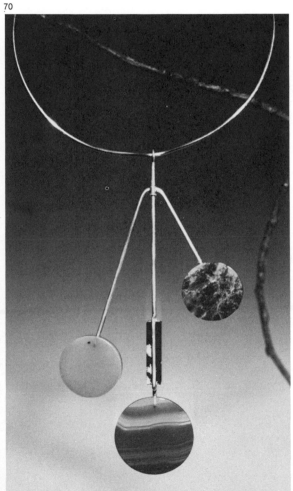

71. Silver pendants by Tone Vigeland of Norway. Convex, filigreed surfaces are positioned opposite one another to create unusual optical effects. (Courtesy of *Bonytt* magazine.)

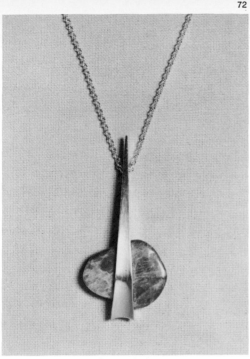

72. Silver pendant with Norwegian sun stone by Øivind Modahl of Norway.

73. Silver pendant with rhodochrosite by Øivind Modahl of Norway. The reverse side of the stone was left raw. Four silver claws hold it in place.

74. Silver pendant with pyrites by Øivind Modahl of Norway. Stones are from the Sulitjelma mine in north Norway.

73

74

75. Pendant by Matti Hyvarinen of Finland. The designer has blended gold, pearls, and Finnish red granite to create this magnificent piece. (Courtesy of Sirokoru.)

76. Fourteen-karat gold pendant by Tapio Wirkkala of Finland. (Courtesy of Westerback Oy.)

77. Fourteen-karat gold pendant by Tapio Wirkkala of Finland. (Courtesy of Westerback Oy.)

76

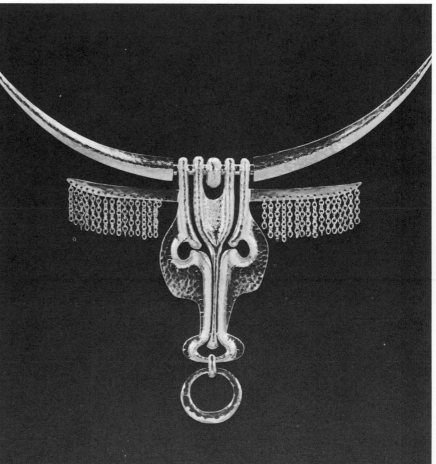

77

78. Necklace in 14-karat gold with textured
surface by Tapio Wirkkala of Finland.
(Courtesy of Westerback Oy.)

78

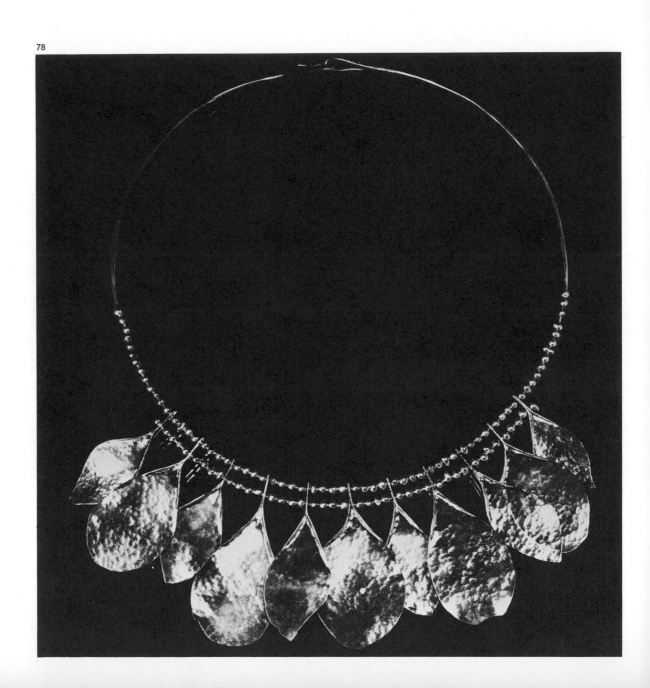

79. Gold necklace with stones of lapis lazuli by Birgitta Haeggbom of Sweden. Small gold balls are used to anchor each suspended form as well as to close the necklace. (Courtesy of Kollegiet for Sverige —Information.)

80. Gold necklace of textured forms by Birgitta Haeggbom of Sweden. (Courtesy of Kollegiet for Sverige—Information.)

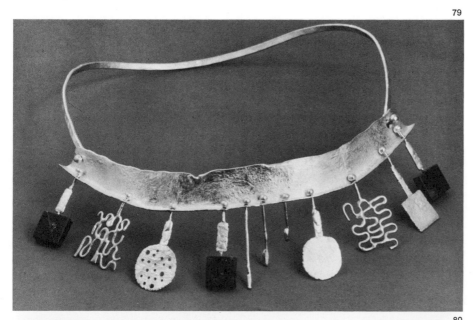

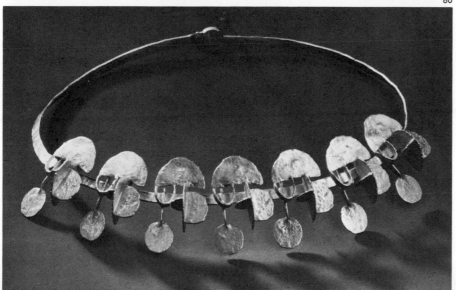

80

81. Sculptured gold pendant with tourmaline by Marianne Aulin and Willy Paldan of Denmark.

82. Textured gold pendant with opal and suspended gold strips. By Marianne Aulin and Willy Paldan of Denmark. The surfaces of the strips are polished smooth to reflect the textured background.

81

82

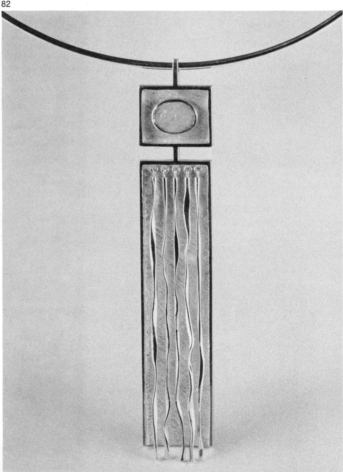

83. Gold necklace with pearls by Birgitta Haeggbom of Sweden. (Courtesy of Kollegiet for Sverige—Information.)

84. Gold necklace by Paula Haivaoja of Finland. (Courtesy of Kalevala Koru and the Finnish Society of Crafts and Design.)

83

84

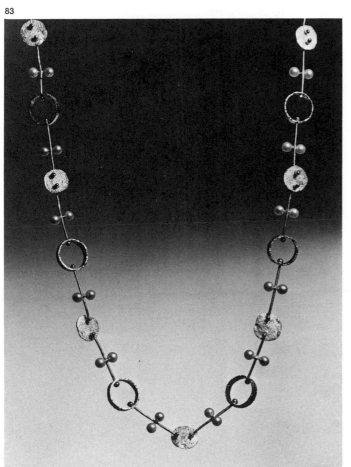

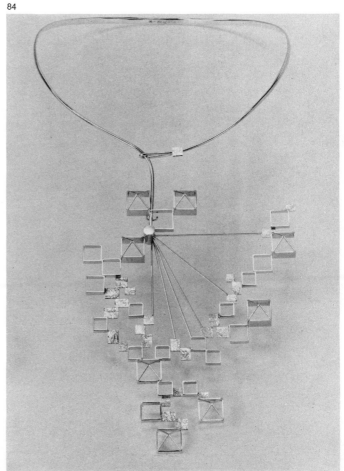

83. Gold necklace with pearls by Birgitta Haeggbom of Sweden. (Courtesy of Kollegiet for Sverige—Information.)

84. Gold necklace by Paula Haivaoja of Finland. (Courtesy of Kalevala Koru and the Finnish Society of Crafts and Design.)

85. Pendant with background of ebony and relief in 14-karat gold. By Poul Warmind of Denmark.

86. "Magic Pearl," pendant in gold by Bjorn Weckstrom of Finland. (Courtesy of Kruunu Koru Oy.)

85

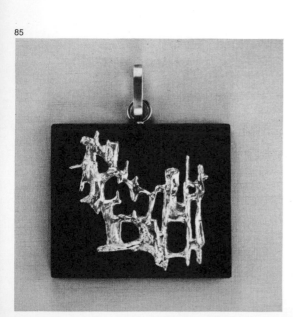

86

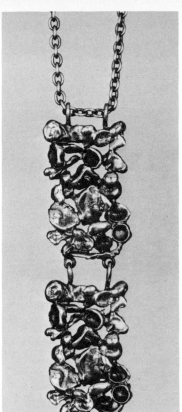

87

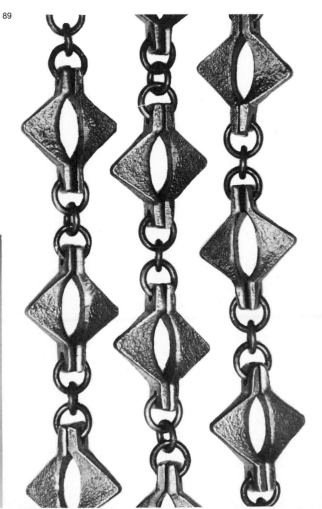

89

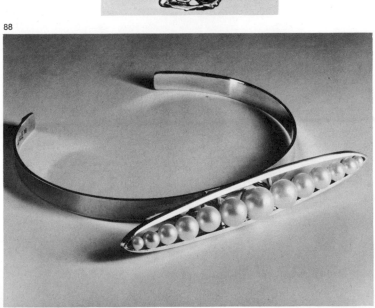

88

87. Sand-cast bronze pendant by Owe Johansson of Sweden. (Courtesy of Kollegiet for Sverige—Information.)

88. Gold collar with pearls by Sigurd Persson of Sweden.

89. Sand-cast bronze necklace by Ibe Dahlquist of Sweden. (Courtesy of Form Design Center in Malmo.)

90. "The Bait," necklace cut from sheet brass by Seppo Tamminen of Finland. (Courtesy of Merkki Sorsa.)

91. Necklace from sheet brass by Seppo Tamminen of Finland. (Courtesy of Merkki Sorsa.)

92. Pendant in brass by Pentti Sarpaneva of Finland. (Courtesy of Kalevala Koru.)

93. Pewter pendant made from wire by Sylvi Levander of Finland. (Courtesy of the Finnish Society of Crafts and Design.)

94. Pendant in brass by Pentti Sarpaneva of Finland. (Courtesy of Turun Hopea.)

95. Pewter pendant made from wire by Sylvi Levander of Finland. (Courtesy of the Finnish Society of Crafts and Design.)

96. Pewter pendant made from wire by Sylvi Levander of Finland. (Courtesy of the Finnish Society of Crafts and Design.)

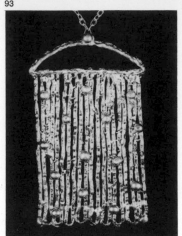

93

94

95

96

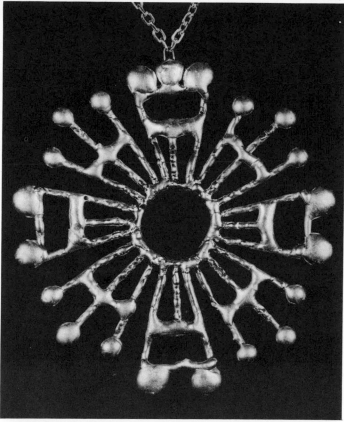

97. Pewter pendant by Sylvi Levander of Finland. (Courtesy of the Finnish Society of Crafts and Design.)

98. Pendant made from pewter wire by Sylvi Levander of Finland. (Courtesy of the Finnish Society of Crafts and Design.)

98

99. Pendant made from pewter wire by Sylvi Levander of Finland. (Courtesy of the Finnish Society of Crafts and Design.)

100. Pendant made from pewter wire by Sylvi Levander of Finland. (Courtesy of the Finnish Society of Crafts and Design.)

99

100

101. Pendant made from textured pewter by Iki Vartiovaara of Finland. (Courtesy of the Finnish Society of Crafts and Design.)

102. Textured pewter pendant by Iki Vartiovaara of Finland. (Courtesy of the Finnish Society of Crafts and Design.)

101

102

103. Cast pewter pendant with leather rawhide necklace by Poul Warmind of Denmark.

104. Cast pewter pendant with leather rawhide necklace by Poul Warmind of Denmark.

103

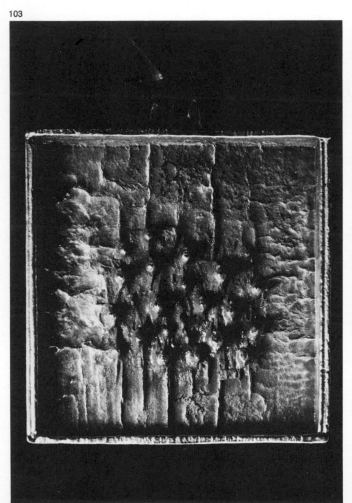

104

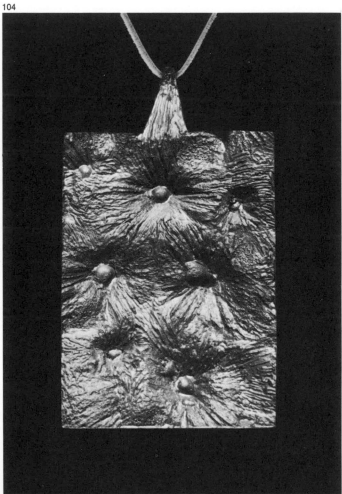

105. Iron pendant by Poul Havgaard of Denmark. All Havgaard's pieces have surfaces of iron polished to a silver color contrasted against iron that has been burned black with cutting oil.

106. Iron pendant by Poul Havgaard of Denmark.

105

106

107. "Tear Drop," pendant of smoke-fired red clay by Catharina Kajander of Finland.

108. Smoke-fired red clay beads by Catharina Kajander of Finland.

109. Leather used as a framing material for pendant stones. By Poulette Manning of Denmark.

107

108

109

110

110. Necklace of green-dyed birch beads by Kaija Aarikka of Finland. The thong used with the beads is leather.

111. Finnish folk necklace of plaited birch bark. The bark was cut into strips, soaked, and then woven into bead forms. (Courtesy of Eila Nevenranta.)

111

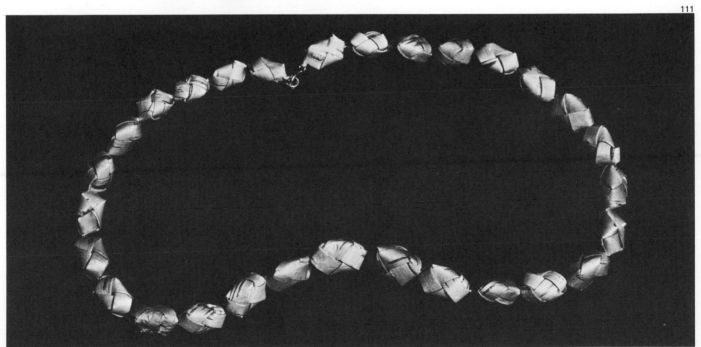

112. Pewter pendants with engravings based on ancient Norwegian rock carvings. By James Moe. (Courtesy of Norsk Design Centrum.)

113. Selection of plastic pendants in contrasting colors by Maija Lavonen of Finland. (Courtesy of Avotakka.)

114. Necklace made from carved cow horn by Bodil Nielsen of Denmark. The black portions of the necklace were made by treating the horn with silver nitrate.

112

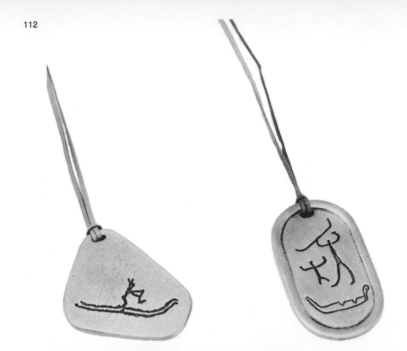

113

114

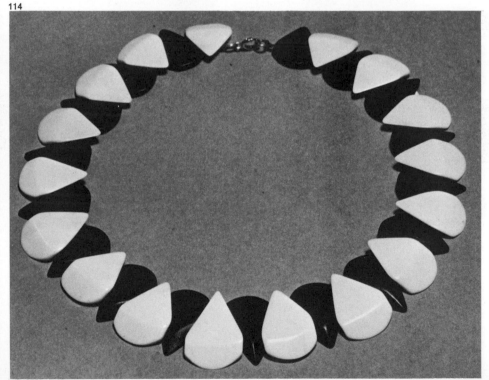

115. Pendants, enamel over copper, by Lase Talosele of Finland. The symbols on these pendants are taken from Lapp ceremonial drums. Called "wizzard" symbols, they are used very frequently by northern Scandinavian designers, both on jewelry and other handcrafted objects.

116. Lapp wizzard symbols. These symbols date from the sixteenth and seventeenth centuries and were painted on drum skins with either blood or the sap from alder bark. (Illustrations by Sandy Willcox.)

116

BRACELETS
AND
ARM BANDS

117. Arm band of folded silver by Bjorn Weckstrom of Finland. An experiment in plasticity, part of the series "Space Sculptures." (Courtesy of Krunnu Koru Oy.)

118. Arm band in folded silver by Bjorn Weckstrom of Finland. (Courtesy of Krunnu Koru Oy.)

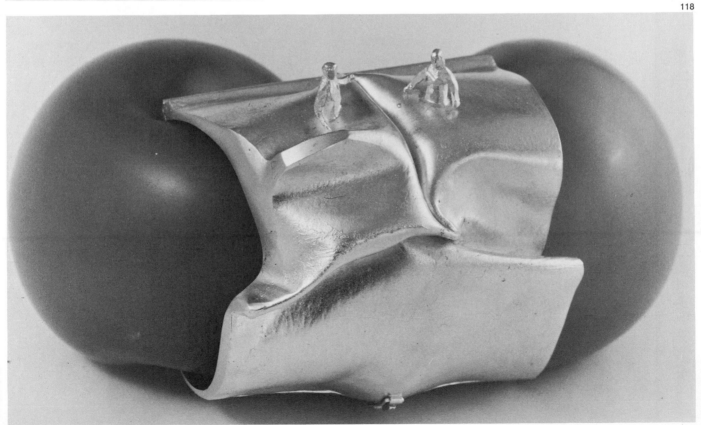

118

119. Arm band in silver with gold plating by Birgitta Haeggbom of Sweden. (Courtesy of Kollegiet for Sverige—Information.)

120. Silver arm band using negative space. By Frank and Regine Juhls of Norway.

121. Constructed silver arm band by Frank and Regine Juhls of Norway.

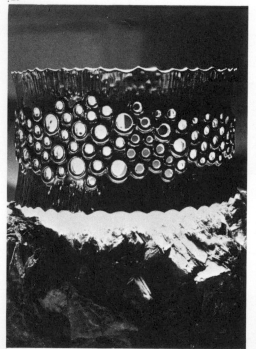

122. Firegilt silver arm band by Bent Gabrielsen Pedersen of Denmark. (Courtesy of Hans Hansen and the Danish Society of Arts and Crafts.)

123. Silver arm band by Frank and Regine Juhls of Norway.

124. Hinged silver bracelet by Owe Johansson of Sweden. (Courtesy of Kollegiet for Sverige—Information.)

123

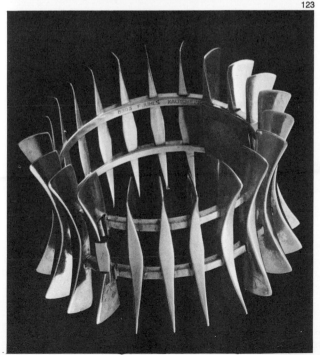

124

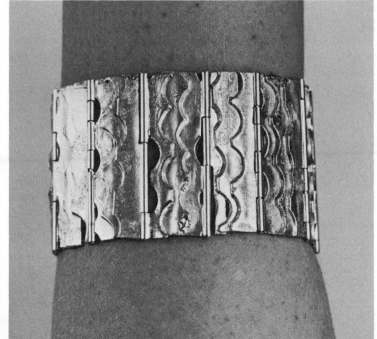

125. Silver arm band by Nanna and Jorgen Ditzel of Denmark. (Courtesy of Georg Jensen Ltd.)

126. Silver bracelet made up of disks. By Bengt Erikson of Finland. (Courtesy of Kalevala Koru.)

127. Expandable arm band in silver by Paula Haivaoja of Finland. (Courtesy of Kalevala Koru and the Finnish Society of Crafts and Design.)

125

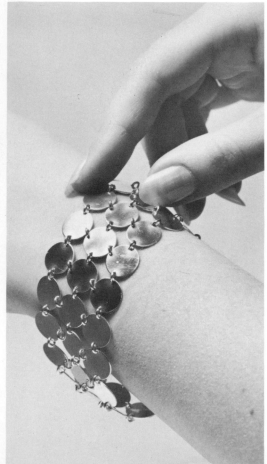

126

127

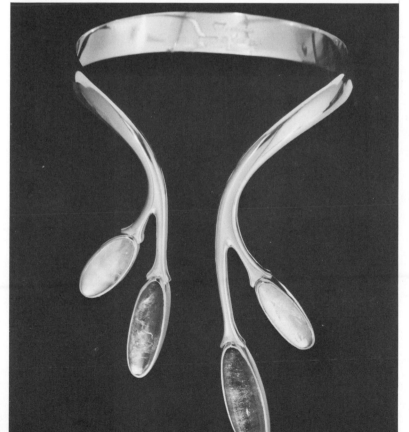

129

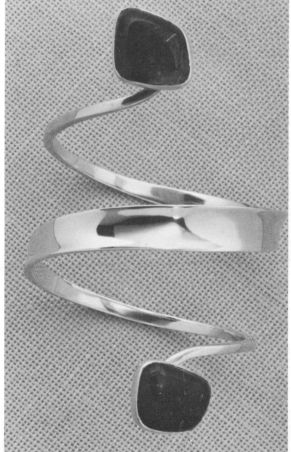

130

128. Silver arm bands with geometric forms. By Anni and Bent Knudsen of Denmark. (Courtesy of the Royal Danish Ministry for Foreign Affairs.)

129. Arm band in silver with berg crystals and citrines. By Theresia Hvorslev of Sweden. (Courtesy of Svenska Slojdforeningen.)

130. Arm band of silver with berg crystals. By Claes E. Giertta of Sweden. (Courtesy of Konstindustriskolan, Goteborg.)

131. Gold bracelet by Tapio Wirkkala of Finland. The negative space contrasts with textured surface. (Courtesy of Westerback Oy.)

132. Gold arm band by Tapio Wirkkala of Finland. (Courtesy of Westerback Oy.)

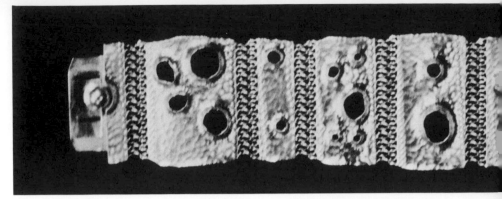

131

132

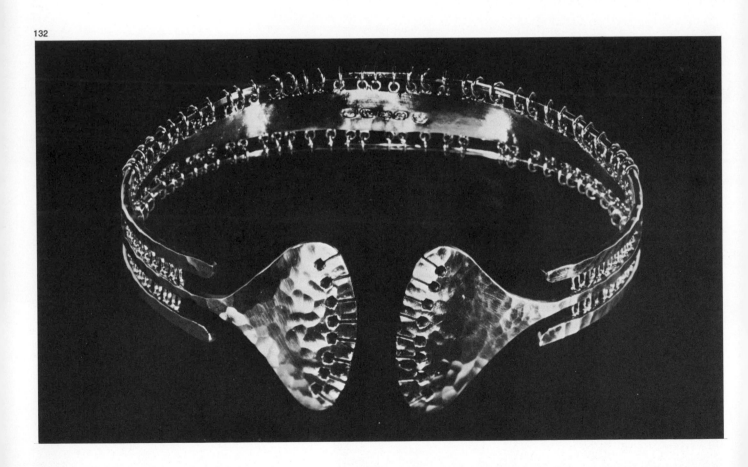

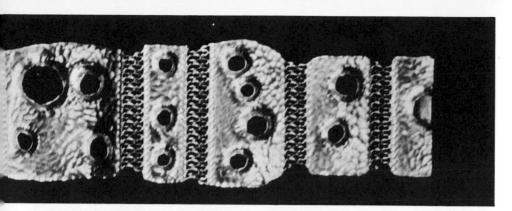

133. Fourteen-karat gold arm band with brilliant-cut diamonds in palladium setting. By Elis Kauppi of Finland. (Courtesy of Kupitaan Kulta Oy.)

133

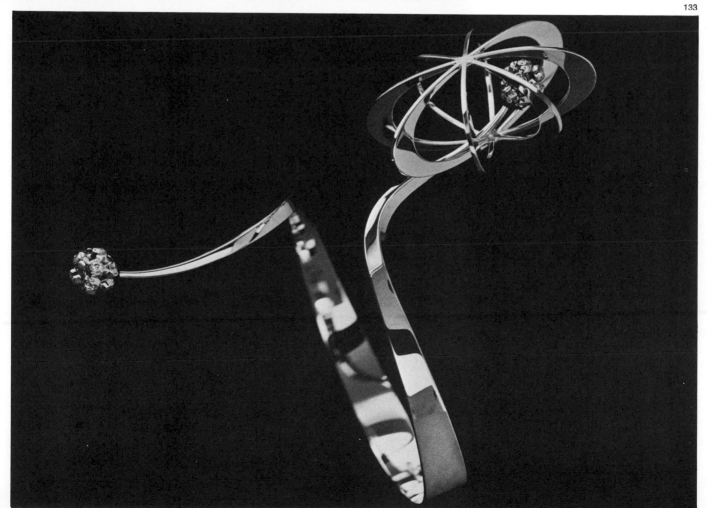

134. Iron arm band by Poul Havgaard of Denmark. This piece is designed to be worn high up on the arm.

135. Gold arm band with brilliant by Sigurd Persson of Sweden. (Courtesy of Svenska Slojdforeningen.)

136. Cast bronze bracelet by Owe Johansson of Sweden. (Courtesy of Kollegiet for Sverige —Information.)

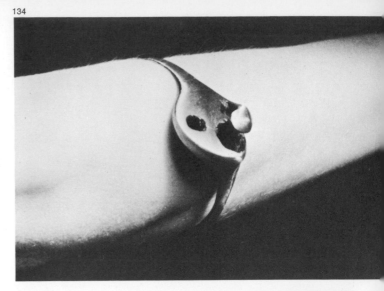

135

136

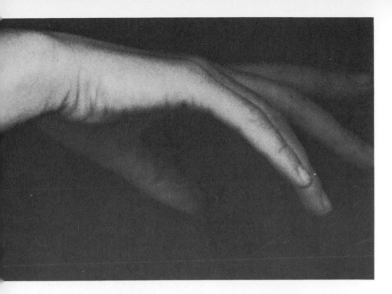

137. Leather arm band by Joe Ortiz of Denmark. The raised design in the center was made by wetting and molding the leather.

137

BROOCHES
AND
PINS

138. Brooch in gold with pearls and
sapphires. By Birgitta Haeggbom of Sweden.
(Courtesy of Kollegiet for Sverige—
Information.)

139. Silver pin using circular slits of
decreasing size to create illusion of great
depth. By Tone Vigeland of Norway.
(Courtesy of Norway Designs.)

140. Silver brooch plated with 24-karat gold
and containing pearls in a deeply textured
surface. By Birgitta Haeggbom of Sweden.
(Courtesy of Kollegiet for Sverige—
Information.)

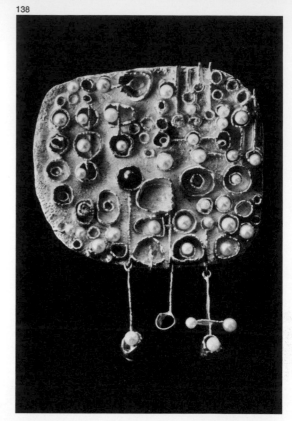

138

139

140

142. Brooch of silver and gold with pearls by
Olle Ohlsson of Sweden. (Courtesy of
Kollegiet for Sverige—Information.)

142

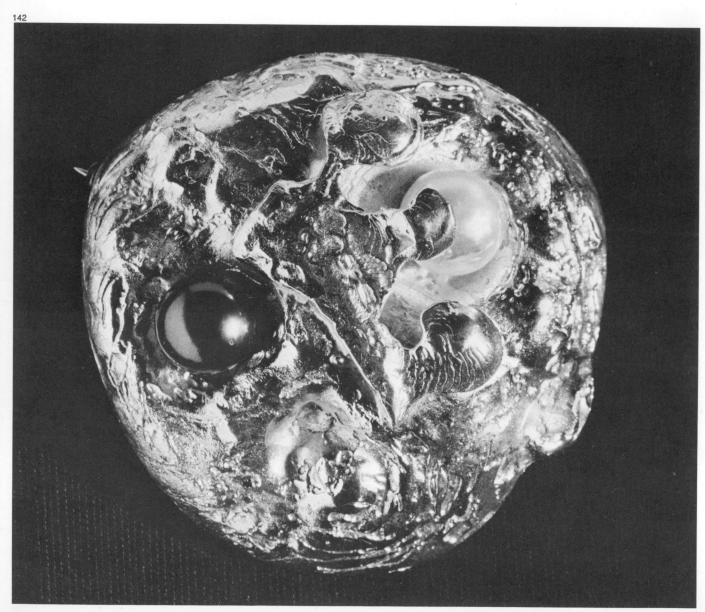

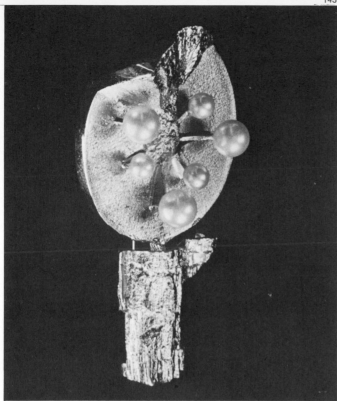

143. "Sea Flower," sculptured gold brooch with pearls by Bjorn Weckstrom of Finland. (Courtesy of the Finnish Society of Crafts and Design.)

144. Textured gold brooch with one pearl by Bjorn Weckstrom of Finland. (Courtesy of the Finnish Society of Crafts and Design.)

145. "Butterfly," brooch combining gold, pearls, and red granite. By Matti Hyvarinen of Finland. (Courtesy of Sirokoru.)

146. Silver brooch by Bjorn Weckstrom of Finland. A vivid example of explosive surface treatment. (Courtesy of the Finnish Design Center.)

147. Brooch in gold by Marianne Aulin and Willy Paldan of Denmark. The irregular holes were burned through the gold and then oxidized at the edges.

146

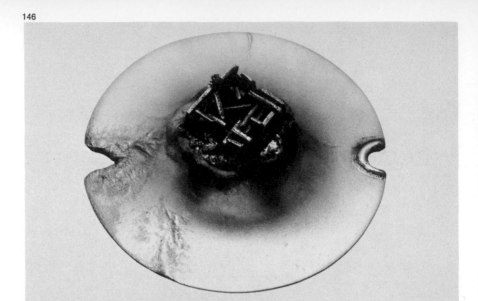

147

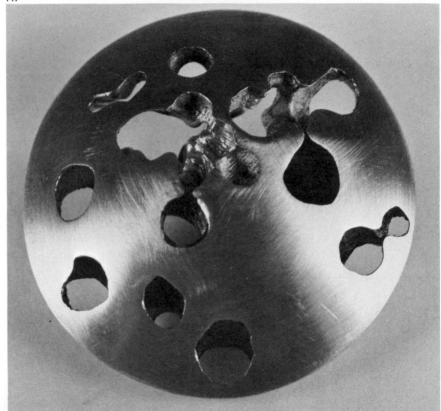

148. Eighteen-karat gold brooch with one black pearl, by Kerstin Ohlin Lejonklou of Sweden. (Courtesy of Kollegiet for Sverige—Information.)

149. Fourteen-karat gold brooch with brilliant-cut diamonds in palladium setting. By Elis Kauppi of Finland. (Courtesy of Kupittaan Kulta Oy.)

149

150. Hammered gold pins by Aulis Blomstedt of Finland. (Courtesy of the Finnish Society of Crafts and Design.)

151. Brooch made of plaited birch root by Ellen Andersson-Kitok of Swedish Lapland. This root material is normally used by the Lapps for weaving baskets. The roots must be drawn, washed, and boiled before they are plaited.

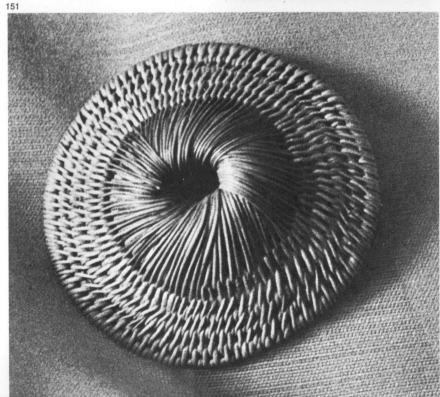

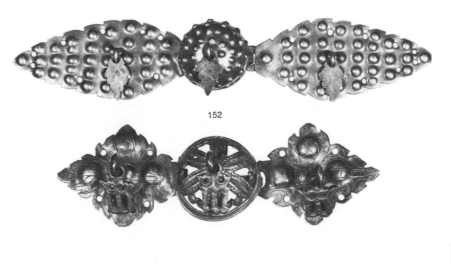

152

152. Silver Lapp fastening devices. These are used in place of buttons and are worn by both men and women on blouses and shirts, as well as sweaters and outer garments. (Courtesy of the National Museum of Finland.)

153. Silver Lapp pins: (a) two from the National Museum of Finland; (b) a reproduction by Frank Juhls of Norway.

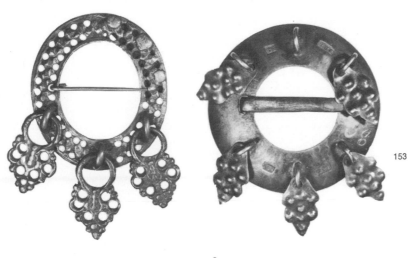

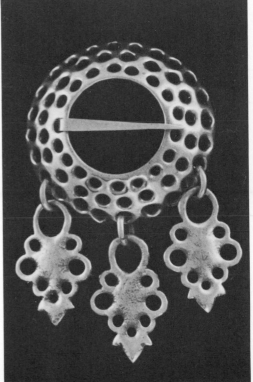

153

a

b

154. Two traditional Lapp brooches in silver by Frank and Regine Juhls of Norway. These brooches are still being worn daily with the colorful costumes of the Norwegian Lapps. The many silver disks are suspended to jingle freely and reflect light.

154

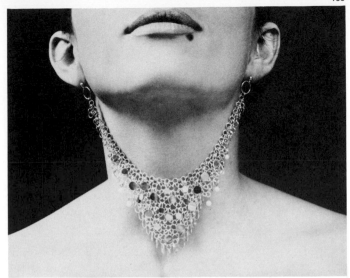

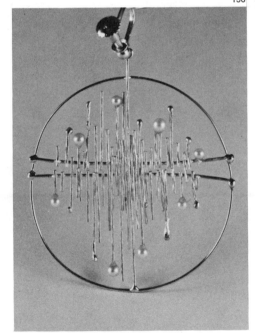

EARRINGS

155. "Double-trouble," ear jewels in 14-karat gold with gold-framed pearls. By Tone Vigeland of Norway. (Courtesy of *Bonytt* magazine.)

156. Earrings of gold and pearls by Marianne Aulin and Willy Paldan of Denmark.

157. Ear jewels in gold with lapis lazuli by Birgitta Haeggbom of Sweden. (Courtesy of Kollegiet for Sverige—Information.)

158. Free-form silver earrings by Regine
Juhls of Norway. Another illustration of the
plasticity of silver.

159. Earrings built from silver wire by
Pentti Sarpaneva of Finland. (Courtesy of
Turun Hopea.)

160. Free-form earrings in silver by Regine
Juhls of Norway.

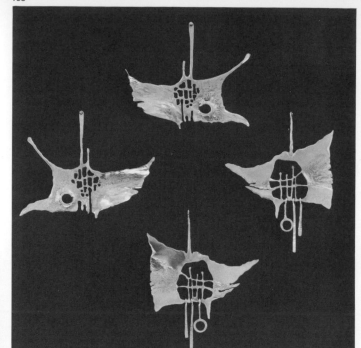

160

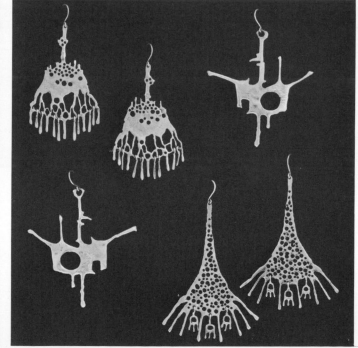

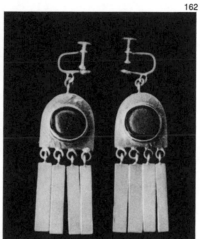

162

161. Silver earrings by Elis Kauppi of Finland. (Courtesy of Kupittaan Kulta Oy.)

162. Silver earrings with beach stones by Tapio Korpisaari of Finland.

163. Sculptured gold earring by Poul Warmind of Denmark.

164. Earrings made from bands of looped silver. By Mirjam Salminen of Finland. (Courtesy of Kaunis Koru Oy.)

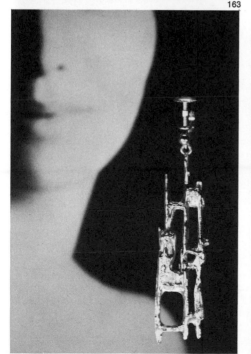

163

164

165. Pine earrings with brass findings by Kaija Aarikka of Finland. The wooden beads are buffed with paraffin wax after being stained.

166. Gold earrings with balls and chains by Tapio Wirkkala of Finland. (Courtesy of Westerback Oy.)

167. Sculptured earrings sand-cast in bronze by Owe Johansson of Sweden. (Courtesy of Kollegiet for Sverige—Information.)

168. Earrings of stained birch beads and brass findings. By Kaija Aarikka of Finland.

166

167

168

169

HEAD ORNAMENTS

169. Hair band made from silver wire and gold beads by Paula Haivaoja of Finland. Tension keeps the band in position. (Courtesy of Kalevala Koru.)

170. Head piece in silver with hammered bands, chains, and balls. By Ylwa Osthall of Sweden. (Courtesy of Konstindustriskolan, Goteborg.)

171. Earring and hair piece combination by Cecilia Johansson of Sweden. Made from silver, silver chain, and beads. (Courtesy of Konstindustriskolan, Goteborg.)

170

171

172. Lapp bridal crown from plaited birch root. By Margit-Astrom Kitok of Sweden. (Courtesy of Pal-Nils Nilsson.)

173. Pony-tail ties crocheted from wool and decorated with dyed wooden beads. By Evelyn Noval of Denmark.

174. Four-strand braided leather hair band. By James Manning of Denmark.

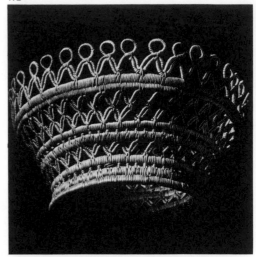

173

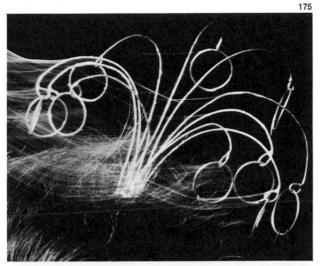

175

176

177

175. Silver crown made from silver wire by Pirkko Lahteenmaki of Finland.

176. Silver crown made from silver wire by Pirkko Lahteenmaki of Finland.

177. "Paribanu's Tears," a "facelet" by Arje Griegst of Denmark. This piece is constructed from gold, with pendants of pearls, emeralds, rubies, and sapphires. (Courtesy of the Royal Danish Ministry of Foreign Affairs.)

BUCKLES
AND
BODY JEWELRY

178. Lapp horn buckle (detail). (Courtesy of
Pal-Nils Nilsson and Nordiska Museet,
Stockholm.)

179. Selection of traditional Lapp buckles
made from reindeer horn. Horn is turned
white by blanching it in a stream, often for
as long as three years. The Lapp also uses
horn in natural color—pink, freshly cut horn,
and old horn which has turned green. These
buckles were rubbed with sedge grass,
engraved, and then stained with a dye made
from water and powdered alder bark.
(Courtesy of Nordiska Museet, Stockholm and
Pal-Nils Nilsson.)

180. Brass buckles cut from sheet brass. By
Seppo Tamminen of Finland. Each buckle is
slightly bent to fit the waist. (Courtesy of
Merkkikeskus Sorsa.)

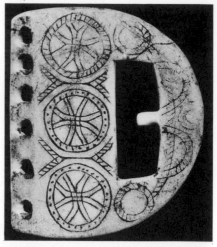

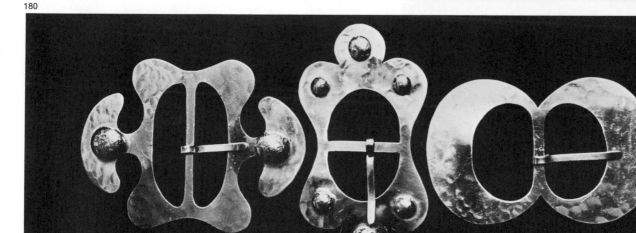

181

182

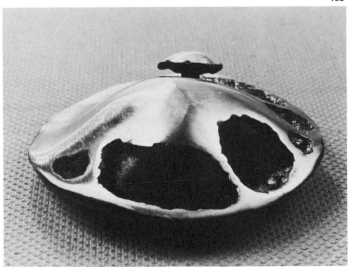

183

184

181. Iron buckle by Poul Havgaard of Denmark. Negative space allows belt leather to show through.

182. Free-form iron buckle by Poul Havgaard of Denmark.

183. Free-form iron buckle by Poul Havgaard of Denmark. This form was hollowed in the center to reduce its weight.

184. Sculptured buckle by Poul Havgaard of Denmark.

185. Leather "snake" belt by James Manning of Denmark.

186. Iron buckle by Poul Havgaard of Denmark. The form was cut from sheet iron with an acetylene torch. As it was cut, the molten iron was allowed to spatter to create the pitted surface.

187. Iron buckle by Poul Havgaard of Denmark. The buckle bar and closing stud are concealed on the reverse side to give the front an uninterrupted surface.

185

186

187

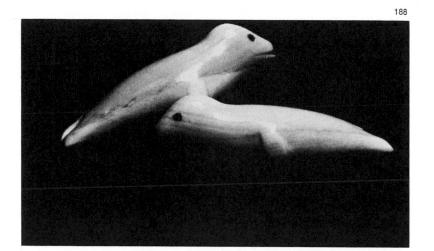

188. Seal buttons carved from whale tooth. (Courtesy of the Danish Handicraft Guild.)

189. Lapp belt-hanger buckle in bronze. It was used to hang knives, scissors, and needles on the belt. (Courtesy of the National Museum of Finland.)

189

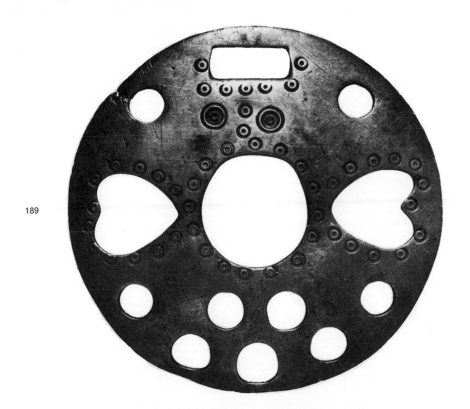

190. Iron breast piece by Poul Havgaard of Denmark.

191. "Belly Sculpture" in iron by Poul Havgaard of Denmark.

192. Free-form iron breast piece by Poul Havgaard of Denmark. This piece is surprisingly light in weight because of the thin-gauge iron used in its construction.

193. Iron breast piece by Poul Havgaard of Denmark. The rough form was cut from sheet iron with an acetylene torch.

190

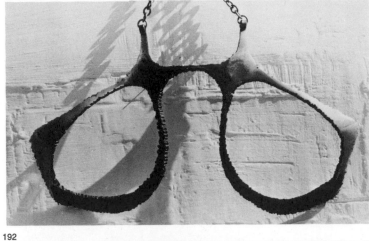

191

192

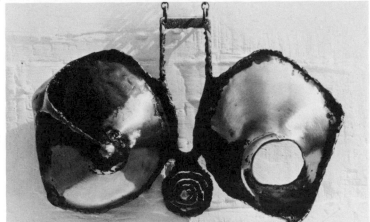

193

MEN'S JEWELRY

194. Antie in silver by Pirkko Lahteenmaki of Finland. (Courtesy of the Finnish Society of Crafts and Design.)

195. Antie in oxidized silver by Thor Selzer of Denmark. (Courtesy of Den Permanente.)

196. Antie in 14-karat gold with four brilliants by Thor Selzer of Denmark. (Courtesy of Den Permanente.)

195

196

197. Oxidized silver cuff links by a student at the Finnish Design School.

198. Silver cuff links by David Andersen of Norway. (Courtesy of Norsk Design Centrum.)

199. Gold cuff links with pyrites mounted uncut. By Øivind Modahl of Norway.

200. "Mountains and Culls," gold cuff links by Bjorn Weckstrom of Finland. Here we see that sculpture is even being extended to cuff links. (Courtesy of Krunnu Koru Oy.)

197

199

198

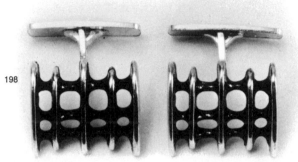

200

201. Detailed drawings for jewelry by Matti Hyvarinen of Finland: (a) brooch to be made with diamonds set in spires of white gold over cast yellow gold and turquoise; (b) ring to be made from cast gold, pearls, diamonds, and white gold; (c) ring to be made of cast gold, diamonds, and a Brazilian stone in its natural form; (d) brooch to be made from diamonds, white gold, yellow gold, and pearls; (e) brooch to be made from diamonds set in white gold on one side, and cast yellow gold on the other.

201

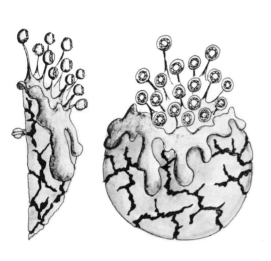

a

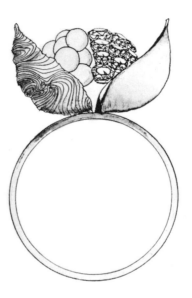

b

c

d

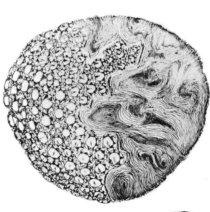

e

ACKNOWLEDGMENTS

In addition to the many craftsmen who contributed to this book, I would like to thank the following organizations and individuals who made my research in Scandinavia possible: Maire Walden and the Finnish Press Bureau; Erkki Savolainen and *Look at Finland* magazine; Sinikka Salokorpi and *Avotakka* magazine; the Finnish Design Center and Reino Routamo; the Finnish Society of Crafts and Design and H. O. Gummerus; Ornamo; the National Museum of Finland; and Eila Nevenranta, Kaj Franck, Howard Smith, Matti Timola, and Catharina Kajander—all of Finland. Norsk Design Centrum, Alf Bøe, and Janicke Meyer; *Bonytt* magazine; Landsforbundet Norsk Brukskunst; Siri Blackstad; and Dr. and Mrs. Peter Anker—all of Norway. The Swedish Society of Crafts and Design and Birgitta Willen; the Swedish Institute; Anna-Greta Erkner Annerfalk and Kollegiet for Sverige—Information; Claes-Hokan Wihl, his wife, and the staff at Monsanto Scandinavia Ab; *Sweden Now* magazine; Pal-Nils Nilsson; Hemslojdforbundet for Sverige; Konstindustriskolan, Goteborg; Nordiska Museet, Stockholm; Historiska Museet, Stockholm; *Forum* magazine; and the Form Design Center in Malmo—all of Sweden. The Danish Society of Arts, Crafts, and Industrial Design, Bengt Salicath, and Aksel Dahl; the Danish Handicraft Guild, Gertie Wandel, and Hanne Zahle; Den Permanente and Mrs. Ole Wanscher; the Royal Danish Ministry of Foreign Affairs Press Office; *Mobilia* magazine; the Danish Handicraft School; and Marianne Aulin, Willy Paldan, John Allpass, Inge Kraus, Kirsten Dehlholm, Birgit Rastrup-Larsen, James Manning, Helle Olsen, Ove Hector Nielsen, Sandy Willcox, and Mr. and Mrs. Kaj Larsen—all of Denmark.

For travel arrangements, I would like to thank: the Finnish Travel Association and Mrs. Bengt Pihlstrom; Finnair; Oy Finnlines Ab; the Finnish Steamship Company; Bore Lines Ab; the Foreign Ministry of Norway; the Norwegian State Railway; Scandinavian Airlines System; the Swedish State Railway; Swedish American Line; the Danish State Railway; the Royal Danish Ministry of Foreign Affairs; and the United Steamship Company of Denmark.

I would like to thank the following photographers and agencies who have work included in this volume: Ilmari Kostiainen; Petrelius; Kristian Runeberg and Seppo Saves; Finn 7; Valokuva-arkisto; Norman Nicholls; Studio Laakso; Studio Rex; J. P. Utanen; Otso Pietinen; Winfrid Zakowski; Rainer Johansson; Sven Raidan; Studio Ulla Finnila; Matti Hyvarinen; Studio Wendt; Fehrmann Ky; Sakari Rimminen; Kuvaus; A. Fothulda and Kalle Kultala—all of Finland. Rolph Grude; Arne Svendsen; Dan Young; Tiegens Foto; Peter Lindholm; Bjorn Rines; Bjorn Østern; Nils Neste; and O. Vaering—all of Norway. Pal-Nils Nilsson/Tio; Bernt Carlzon; Jan Olsson; Sorvik; Bengt Carlen; AB Nordiska Kompaniet; Sundahl; Peter Zimberg; Reijo Ruster; Arne Enander; Atelje Visit; and Birger Haglund—all of Sweden. Anne Havgaard; Rigmore Mydtskov and Steen Bønne; Jonals Foto; Juncker Studio; Ove Hector Nielsen; Peter Borup Laursen; Jan Selzer; Louis Schnakenburg; Jørn Freddie; and Claus Koefoed—all of Denmark.

MATERIALS FOR FURTHER STUDY

The following books and periodicals may be ordered directly from their publishers in Europe and the United States:

Avotakka (periodical), Salomonkatu 17-A, Helsinki 10, Finland.
Designed in Finland (annual), Finnish Foreign Trade Association, Et Esplanadikatu 18, Helsinki 13, Finland.
Haycraft, John, *Finnish Jewelry and Silverware,* Otava Publishing Co., Uudenmaankatu 8-12, Helsinki, Finland (1962).
Look at Finland (periodical), Finnish Travel Association, Foreign Department, Mikonkatu 13-1, Helsinki, Finland.
SDO (newspaper), Scandinavian Design Students' Organization, Ateneum, Railroad Square, Helsinki, Finland.

Bonytt (periodical), Bygdoy Alle 9, Oslo 2, Norway.
Gullsmed Kunst (periodical), Storgate 14, Oslo 1, Norway.
Norsk Husflid (periodical), Ø Slottsgate 8, Oslo 1, Norway.
Norsk Kunsthandverk, Bonytt Publishing Co., Bygdoy Alle 9, Oslo 2, Norway (1968).

Forum (periodical), Box 7047, Stockholm 7, Sweden.
Handicraft in Sweden, Svenska Hemslojdsforeningarnas Riksforbund, Sturegatan 29, 11129 Stockholm, Sweden.
Hemslojden (periodical), Brannkyrkagatan 117, Stockholm, Sweden.

Holmquist, Kersti, and Grundstrom, Ake, *Nineteenth Century Brass,* Nordiska Museet, Stockholm, Sweden (1967).
Lillecrona, Gull, *Swedish Handicraft,* Swedish Institute, P.O. Box 7072, 10382, Stockholm, Sweden.
Pettersons, Victor, *Design in Scandinavia,* Bokindustri Ab, Stockholm, Sweden (1968).
Sweden Now (periodical), Warfvinges Vag 26, Stockholm, Sweden.
Widman, Dag, *Swedish Design,* Swedish Institute, P.O. Box 7072, 10382 Stockholm, Sweden.
—————. *Swedish Handicraft,* Raben & Sjogrew, Stockholm, Sweden (1967).

The Arts of Denmark, Viking to Modern, Danish Society of Arts, Crafts, and Industrial Design, Bredgade 58, 1260 Copenhagen K, Denmark (1960).
Contemporary Danish Design, Danish Society of Arts, Crafts, and Industrial Design, Bredgade 58, 1260 Copenhagen K, Denmark.
Lassen, Erik, *Danish Silver,* Thaning & Appels Forlag, Copenhagen, Denmark (1964).
Dansk Kunsthaandvaerk (periodical), Danish Society of Arts, Crafts, and Industrial Design, Bredgade 58, 1260 Copenhagen K, Denmark.
Denmark Review (periodical), Ministry of Foreign Affairs, Christiansborg, Copenhagen, Denmark.
Guldsmedebladet (periodical), Ryvangs Alle 26, 2100 Copenhagen Ø, Denmark.

Haandarbejdets Fremme, Danish Handicraft Guild, Vimmelskaftet 38, Copenhagen K, Denmark.
Hioit, Esbjørn, *Modern Danish Silver,* Jul. Gjellerups Forlag, Copenhagen, Denmark (1954).
Kaufmann, Edgar, Jr., Lassen, Erik, and Raventlow, Charles Ditlev, *Fifty Years of Silver in the Georg Jensen Tradition,* Georg Jensen Silversmiths, Copenhagen, Denmark (1954).
Lassen, Erik, *Danish Knives, Forks, and Spoons,* Host & Sons Forlag, Copenhagen, Denmark (1960).
Lubecker, Pierre, *Kaj Bojesen Silversmith,* Danish Society of Arts, Crafts, and Industrial Design, Bredgade 58, 1260 Copenhagen K, Denmark (1955).
Mobilia (periodical), Snekkersten, Denmark.
Møller, Svend Erik, *34 Scandinavian Designers,* Mobilia, Snekkersten, Denmark (1967).
Møller, Viggo Sten, *Henning Koppel* (Danish silver design), Rhodos, Copenhagen, Denmark (1965).
Scandinavian Times Magazine, Kompagnlstraede 39, 1208 Copenhagen K, Denmark.
A Treasury of Scandinavian Design, Hassings Forlag As, Vodroffsvej 26, Copenhagen, Denmark (1961).

The American Scandinavian Review, American Scandinavian Foundation, 127 E. 73 St., New York, N.Y. 10021.
Andren, Erik, *Swedish Silver,* Barrows, M. & Co., New York, N.Y. (1950).

Plath, Iona, *The Decorative Arts of Sweden,* Charles Scribner's Sons, New York (1948).

Hall, Wendy, *The Finns and Their Country,* Max Parrish & Co., 2 Portman Street, London W1, England (1967). Segerstad, Ulf Hard af, *Scandinavian Design,* Studio Books, London, England (1961).

The following Scandinavian schools offer courses in jewelry-making:

Ateneum, Railway Square, Helsinki 10, Finland

Statens Handverks og Kunstindustri-skole, Ullevalsvejen 5, Oslo 1, Norway Statens Kunstindustriskole, Bergen, Norway

Konstfackskolan, Valhallavegen 191, Stockholm, Sweden Konstindustriskolan, Kristinelundsgatan 6-8, Goteborg C, Sweden

Kunsthaandvaerkskolan, Copenhagen, Denmark The Royal Danish Academy, Kongens Nytorv 1, Copenhagen, Denmark

Scandinavian design and handicraft societies and exhibitions:

The Finnish Design Center, Kasarmin-katu 19, Helsinki, Finland The Finnish Society of Crafts and Design, Unionkatu 30, Helsinki 10, Finland Ornamo, Ainonkatu 3, Helsinki 10, Finland

Landsforbundet Norsk Brukskunst, Uranienborgvejen 2, Oslo 1, Norway Norsk Design Centrum, Drammensvejen 40, Oslo 2, Norway

The National Association of Swedish Handicraft Societies, Mimervagen 8, Djursholm 2, Sweden Svenska Slojdforeningen, Nybrogatan 7, Box 7047, Stockholm 7, Sweden

The Danish Handicraft Guild, Vimmels-kaftet 38, Copenhagen K, Denmark The Danish Society of Arts, Crafts, and Industrial Design, Bredgade 58, 1260 Copenhagen K, Denmark Den Permanente, Vesterport, Copen-hagen, Denmark